U.S.A.

CRISIS SOLVED

SERGIO GUADARRAMA

ISBN: 1494407590
ISBN 13: 9781494407599

CHAPTER I

THE POWER OF FAITH IN GOD

My God will bless you and your family with wisdom and direction, and He will provide you with divine protection.

S. G.

Faith in God, Ali Baba, or whomever your celestial protector is; faith in yourself; and hope and faith in your country is all it takes. The only road that assures us of anything is the road of faith in God—nothing more and nothing less. Because the world exists of good and bad, we need to stay on the right road, the one of faith in God. God's road is very narrow, and rarely traveled. Most people prefer the easy route: wide, multi-lane highways that making getting on and off simple. The easy way, however, is the wrong way. It has no sense of direction, no single-minded purpose. These highways have too many exits, many leading to substance abuse or crime. God's way is a little more difficult to follow, and you need to believe it is the right way for you and your family. But, every mile you travel will teach you something new—and at the same time, give you faith, strength, and purpose. This is the real path; where at the end something special awaits you and your family.

True faith in God is like an airplane. A plane is airborne as soon as it leaves the ground; from the runway to the sky is a straight line. It does not go up and down during flight or change course midair unless an emergency arises. Who knows where the plane will end up—maybe on an island in paradise or on another continent. Yet no matter where the plane lands, it always goes forward. That is God's way.

When the pilot starts moving his plane down the runway, with close to 400 people on board, he must have faith that everything will go well with the takeoff and landing. He must believe in God. If he does not have faith, all those 400 people aboard had better start praying. It is a good idea to pray anyway, just to make sure. Every day, tens of thousands of people travel by commercial airplanes in thousands of flights; most of the time, the planes land safely. Yet once in a while accidents occur. We could say this is destiny, because the planes are so safe . . . most of the time. But, the possibility always exists.

The same is true with car accidents. The best thing we can do to minimize accidents is to pray to avoid them, and be well prepared so that preventable disasters can be eluded. God gives us the knowledge to do the best in a tough situation. Every day, new advances in technology emerge making planes and cars safer for passengers. At the same time, however, the risk of human error can never be eliminated. Every day, people face challenging situations like snow, thunderstorms, heavy rain, and the like. Emergencies happen without notice, and that is when you need to rely on God and His wisdom to see you safely through.

My parents went to school for only a few early years, through the elementary grades. After they got married, they dedicated their entire lives to supporting their family. There were nine of us: six boys and three girls. We grew up in a small town in Mexico; back then it was called Villa Acuna. It was right on the border with Del Rio, Texas. One time in Del Rio, a friend of my father's who owned several gas stations, asked my father, "Why do you drive that old truck? You do not drink or smoke. You work hard and earn good money. You could buy a Cadillac." The man was amazed my father would put all his money and effort, and his faith, in his children. This rich man had only one son, and that son never made it to college.

With my father's persistence, three of his sons graduated. It was a major accomplishment for a small-town family. The girls all finished middle school, but back then, college was not an option, as the nearest one was over 300 miles away.

My parents were able to achieve this for our family because of their faith in God and love for their children. They are like many families around the world who love and support their children, and have hopes of a better life for them. They sacrifice and have faith that Jesus will give wisdom and protection, guidance and direction.

When soldiers board the plane that will take them to combat, the first thing they do after bidding farewell to their loved ones is to pray. They leave everything in the hands of God, and have faith they will return to their families soon. Many return, but many do not because it is their destiny to become a casualty of war. Only God knows why such a thing happens, why such a situation is happening right now, in Afghanistan. The decision to be a soldier might have been made long before the soldier leaves home, but the family starts praying for their loved one's protection right away. They firmly believe God will answer their prayers, even in the most dangerous situations.

The war on terrorism is not an easy one. The stronger the faith and the more earnest the prayers, the better the result we see on the battleground, where any small error can turn fatal. Even though the military tries to control the situation, it is very dangerous and unpredictable for the soldiers because they cannot tell their friends from foes. We should help such war-ridden countries like Iraq and Afghanistan; and as soon as they can defend themselves, we must leave them to self-govern. Wars are not worth prolonging past that stage. The sacrifice of our soldiers' lives is too great. It is like running in the Olympics without a reward—but the bullets still fly, and our soldiers still die.

Imagine the astronaut who knows two space missions have ended in disaster, and the smallest glitch with takeoff or reentry into the earth's atmosphere can be fatal. Faith is what helps them maintain the extraordinary level of alertness and focus necessary to complete the mission. Even then, only God knows the astronaut's destiny. These brave men and women are aware of the risk, and they know they are in God's hands from the moment the mission begins. The preparation of any voyage is planned to the last detail to avoid the risk of accidents, because the engineers know any error in their calculations can have grave consequences. They not only prepare physically but also spiritually, because they know their faith in God and Jesus is the most important preparation they can make to safely return to Earth. The spiritual training must begin at the beginning, before the countdown to launch. Once the countdown begins, no one can guarantee a safe return; but, if all have abundant faith in God, they will have a safe landing.

When the astronauts depart, they go into the unknown. They trust the engineers, who also have faith in the project. The engineers at the Space Center strive to be better every time they launch a new mission. As you can see, it is a chain of faith. All the people involved are part of the chain: the astronauts, engineers, other workers, family, friends, and fellow countrymen—everyone around the world, all in one prayer to God to protect the astronauts throughout their journey and back again to Earth.

In sports, from the time athletes play their first Pee Wee game, to high school, college and beyond, players pray before the game. They believe God will protect them from injuries, and will help them win the game. Most of the time, everything goes well—though sometimes accidents happen, especially in rough sports. God gives the win to the best-prepared team. This goes beyond the game. The players must practice every day to be the best they can be, and they must pray in the name of God to help them. Training is not easy, practice games are not easy, and time off the field is not easy, where people talk judge the players. The players pray to God; they ask for divine help, not only to win but also to finish the game without injury so they can continue to play. That is why players pray, not just at the start of a game, but also at the start of practice. In fact, most pray every day, knowing if they have faith in God, their sports careers will be in good hands; God will answer their prayers. Some athletes do not believe in the power of God, and they disappear before making it big. All the best-known athletes and sports superstars believe in God. They have learned that without faith in God, they could not have reached the top of their sport.

Remember, one's ultimate goal and one's children's goals will be realized if one prays and believes in God. The parents or families of all types of service personnel— Army soldiers, Marines, Air Force pilots, SWAT teams, military police, and regular police—have faith they will return unharmed. But the line of duty is thin, and these courageous men and women risk their lives every day. They pray to God, and the majority returns home safely to their families. Only God knows why some do not return.

Even in risky professions the destiny of everyone in the world plays a major role. In an ordinary city, for example, more people die in accidents than police or soldiers. Why?

Because accidents can happen to anyone, not just soldiers or law enforcement officers. Imagine police officers all across the United States making thousands of routine stops or respond to 911 calls, each time facing the unknown. Some of these encounters end in shootings and chases that endanger not only the police, but also innocent victims along the way.

Soldiers help defend us in peacetime, as well as when we are at war. With one ongoing war the chances of our young soldiers dying today have greatly magnified. As citizens, we must pray every day, because—regardless of age, or sex, or profession—these brave folks help us. For example, SWAT teams are trained specifically for diffusing dangerous situations. They respond many times a year, and yet they do not know if they will come back safely.

Do you know how far away Heaven is? I asked an astronomer friend what the secret of the universe was, because he was always busy visiting the observatories of the world and peering into the heavens. He replied, "You are asking the wrong person." Even professionals who routinely discover planets similar to Earth have not seen Paradise. Even if we stay on our planet and visit the best places—Hawaii, Cancun, the Mediterranean, or any other appealing locale—I can tell you God made those places, and our beautiful planet, for us to enjoy. Who will go to Heaven? We do not know. We do know, however, we have the opportunity to enjoy the fruits of God's labor here on Earth.

Astronomers are heading for a revolution, in terms of capacity to see and study space with a new generation of super-telescopes, like the gigantic mega-lenses 80 feet in diameter and Europe's largest telescope, with a diameter of 138 feet. If astronomers still do not see Heaven from Earth, even with these lofty tools, at least they can try to understand some of the biggest secrets of the universe, and perhaps of humankind. New discoveries are being made all the time, and no one knows where they will lead; but one thing is for sure: these discoveries will yield great benefits to science and society. I believe "pre-Heaven" exists on this Earth, and it means living the best life you can with your family and loved ones. If you did everything possible to help those around you, you can say you were living in Heaven on Earth.

When we, or someone we love, go to the hospital, it is not easy on anyone, whether patient, family, or beloved. Research has shown that people who believe in God make better recoveries. God gives us the strength we need. Our faith is, and will forever be, what we must reinforce every day. It gives us strength to face each challenge, even possible death. Pray the doctors perform their jobs well, but 80% of the effort comes from our faith, courage, hope, and determination. This is why praying to God is of utmost importance. We cannot do it alone. We need to know God is watching and will always help in any situation of life or death.

Some patients do not know the right road. Do not feel discouraged because you do not find the right path at first. Have faith in God; in time, you will find the right direction. It is in God's map where you will find your path and your purpose. Faith and purpose must go hand-in-hand, so you can use your own will power and be guided by God toward your purpose.

People without faith in God rarely do good in life because, without a living faith, it is doubly difficult to do anything or be who you really want to be. You need to be straightforward with your faith in God. You need to believe that only by faith will you succeed; there are no two ways around it. You must have faith in yourself; but, first of all, you need faith in God. Only then will God guide you. When we receive God's guidance and wisdom, we know He is on our side. This is what matters in life. You can follow your own path, but I can tell you I have travelled the road of faith in God and I know it is the right way. We already know exercise is good for the body, education is good for the mind, and faith is superb for the soul. If you keep these three things in mind, you have a winning combination.

Always remember faith in God is all it takes. If you have faith in God, He will provide answers to your questions, answers that are straightforward and easy to understand, even in difficult situations. God will always be there for you. Having faith in God increases your odds of living a successful life. Pray every day and try hard to achieve your dreams; God will help you accomplish them. God can remove any obstacle in your way to help you succeed.

If you believe in God, your possibilities in your life are endless. Your prayers and faith in God play the most important roles. They will bring you excitement and enthusiasm, and you will see a wonderful life is waiting for you. If you believe in God, everything is possible. If you do not believe in God, prepare yourself for the consequences. Faith in God is what makes miracles happen, and we must believe God exists in the universe to accomplish great things. Without faith in God, we dare not turn any corners because we do not know if something bad awaits us. With faith, however, we can reverse any negative situations to our favor. God wants the best of the best for us, and we must believe He has great plans for all the good people on the planet.

God has always been good to the American people. This is why there are good and bad people in this world. If we have faith in God, He will open the doors of opportunity and abundance, not only for you but also for our nation. For you to be reading this book is no coincidence. God put this book in your way. This is your opportunity to reaffirm your faith in God. If you believe in God, you will see good things happening to those around you. God wants the best for everybody, and you are no exception. When you choose to have faith in God, He will be ready to help you with your fears, struggles, and challenges. He will always help you look for the best alternatives in life.

You can have good habits and good discipline. If you know how to be humble, faith in God is all you need to handle any defeats life throws your way. You will be better prepared for the hard-boiled challenges life presents. Life, we know, is not like Disneyland; but one thing we know for sure is if we have faith in God, at least life can be handled without difficulty. It is a matter of believing in the wisdom of God. Faith in God is the most important, no matter your religion.

You will be part of a new generation of successful Americans because you have chosen to help your country transform its future. You can start right now, but remember, you need to trust the word of God in everything you do. You already know God wants you to do your best. He has been helping millions of people since the inception of civilization, and He will continue to do so until the end of time. Even if you think the end is near, there are still many years before the end. It is unlikely my own grandchildren will live to see the end. In how many years will Earth be destroyed? No one knows. In the meantime, He will provide us with wisdom and strength. For now, start praying—and the rest will follow.

If you want to have faith but do not know how, it is very simple. Anyone can have faith but first you must believe God is the creator of the universe, that God is everywhere, even inside of us. Faith is mighty. Believing God will help you through any situation is all you need in your life. Remember God will be with you. Be thankful for each moment of our lives we enjoy in the company of our loved ones. When you find your faith in God, teach it to your children. Teach them to pray on a daily basis, and the challenges they face will be easier to confront. The best thing we can do for future generations of Americans is to pass on our faith, hope, and belief; only then we will have a healthy society and vibrant economy.

We need to have faith in our government to turn the economy around. We need to have faith in industries manufacturing American goods, and we must have faith our own people will help achieve our nation's economic goals by buying more Made-in-America products. If we want the United States to be in the forefront of global trade and commerce, we need to start buying our own products—and cease buying those made in any other country. Then we wait, and watch our message reach American companies and our competitors on other shores. We also await the American people's response, to see whether this key to opening the doors of our economy will be used. People can decide whether or not to have faith in America; they can buy American-made goods and help keep that door open, or buy Chinese-made products and watch our economy sink.

I am not saying we should discard our ethnic heritage. If you live in the United States and are Chinese, you can buy made-in-China products. If you are from Colombia, enjoy your Colombian coffee. If you are from Mexico, cook with Mexican ingredients. No one can—or should—tell you not to purchase products made in your home country. We just need to be aware that the more we buy American-made products, the more secure we will feel and the more security we will have in our American lives. It is your decision to buy less expensive goods made cheaply in other countries, but by doing so you jeopardize your job, home, and future. Think twice before you buy products made outside the United States. I do not want you to say later, "I didn't know. Nobody told me."

I can imagine your objections: "But, Sergio, we already know you have faith America can be like it was forty or so years ago. But these days that expectation feels like a "mission impossible" for American manufacturing companies. Competition from China alone competition is so overwhelming we are on the brink of a manufacturing collapse. Our own companies are leaving the United States left and right."

I know. I know if we do not change direction, our home-grown manufacturers will become extinct. We already lost the retail store battle against the Chinese and American companies that are now our competition. Chinese goods now dominate retail stores large and small. The Chinese beat us—but not without the help of some of our own companies, like Apple, Dell, Intel, and thousands of others.

One other thing that bothers me is we are losing when it comes to home improvement. Made-in-America brands are disappearing from the shelves, and you know from what country we see so many products in the orange-and-blue home improvement centers. Things are changing so fast that soon the only American-made product remaining on our shelves will be the lumber the shelves are made from. When that happens, the trade fight will be over. Yet I have faith America will stand out on the canvas once again. We already know what happened in the 1930s, so I do not think it will be impossible.

The solution to improving the American economy is in our own hands. All we need is to have faith in American products, and faith that our government will go the extra mile to help our manufacturing companies fabricate better quality products and improve the existing ones. People will be fully aware that, if we buy plenty of American-made products, the possibilities of a healthy economy increase quickly and steadily. So, if the new generation of made-in-the-U.S.A. products is of a high quality, there is no reason not to buy those goods. From now on, we have the key. If we are proud of America, it is time to buy mainly American-made products, even if, in the beginning, they will be a little more expensive. Their quality, however, will be better and will get even better as time passes by.

So, our faith in U.S.-made products needs to be strong and steady. My mother always said to me, "Never, ever lose your faith in anything that you believe." If we believe in our own nation with our own products, we need to go forth with full faith. There is no room for only half-faith; you either have faith or you do not. We only have two choices: one is to buy mainly U.S.-made products; or two, we could continue with the same trend and soon find out the sad reality that we are at risk of another recession. But, always remember that faith in American products is our main hope.

CHAPTER II

THE MIND OF A
SERIAL KILLER

I do not like to read or write violent horror stories, or watch such movies, because I reject anything non-existent in real life. I see enough violence in the news. If I wanted to write a book about violence, I have plenty of material coming from Mexico, my home country, such as the brutal fighting among the cartels and the Mexican Federal Police for control of drug routes into the United States. The abundance of material could fill many books each year but that is not my style. The last horror film I went to see was when I was a teenager. It was *The Exorcist*, and I decided then that these types of movies do nothing good for your mind. In fact, seeing too many of these types of movies will affect fragile minds, potentially leaving such people more susceptible to fear for the rest of their lives. Scaring easily, they turn smaller problems into larger ones in their mind, which, in turn, can affect their behavior and potentially create a habit of violence. It becomes a vicious circle.

When I was a child, in Mexico, I saw two gunfights in different areas of the city. Each one took place not five yards from where I was standing, so I witnessed everything. I saw who fought and I saw who won. I have been in places considered spooky, but my father always warned me to be careful with living people because the dead do not do you any harm. So, violent movies do not scare me, but I still do not like to watch them because I have better things to see and read.

Once, when I was working at one of my customer's houses, my customer told me about his experience serving in the Army during one of the wars. He had been a machine-gunner in a helicopter, and he had killed many people. I mentioned a new movie that had earned good reviews, to which he responded with a very bad gesture. He said he did not watch war movies because they gave him nightmares; had no interest reliving the horrors of his time in the war.

I knew another ex-soldier who was a baseball player, and a very good one. He had just one problem: If someone yelled something from the stands, he would run from the field, even if he was in the middle of catching the ball. He was suffering from post-traumatic stress disorder, as many soldiers do; they bring the ravages and scars of the war home with them and cannot escape them. Clearly, some come home with horrible physical injuries, including missing limbs, burns that will not heal, or head wounds from which they will never fully recover. These are the real-life, terrible effects of war. These brave men and women sacrifice so much, more than any monetary compensation. It makes no sense to go to war and pay such a heavy price for slight provocation. We need to be very careful and understand real life is not a movie. It is not wise to start another war in the Persian Gulf while we still fight in Afghanistan.

When a serial killer is on the run, law enforcement joins forces at national, state, and municipal levels. When the FBI gets involved, many resources are used, including goods, planes, and helicopters, to conduct widespread searches for victim and killer alike. When the manhunt starts, the authorities know they are up against criminals who can cover their tracks very well. But perpetrators feel they are invincible, superior to the police. This is usually why they make small mistakes that eventually get them caught. One thing is for sure: these criminals are relentless and will not stop willingly. It is the work of the best detectives to look for the smallest detail to start their investigations; they fine-tune their strategies and

skills to find these dangerous assassins on the loose. The police take precautions of their own, so they can keep themselves
and the public safe.

When police look for a serial killer, they put the profile in
perspective for the FBI agents. Behavioral psychologists as-
sisting the police know serial killers are persons who will not
stop killing until they are put behind bars. They try to predict
the serial killer's next moves, and spend many hours looking
for flaws or mistakes the killer may have made. As skilled as
police are, it takes much effort, time, and money to catch these
psychopaths. Luckily, today's technology makes it easier for
the police to catch criminals faster.

When our country is at constant war, where innocent people on all sides get killed, something needs to be done, just
like something needs to be done with the serial killer. Sooner
or later, we are going to suffer the consequences. We need to
be smarter, and use our technologies to defend ourselves from
any bellicose nation. We should live as though war were the
very last resort. It is better to promote peace than to win several wars, even just one war. Waging war as a last resort may at
times be necessary and therefore acceptable; starting a war because of an intelligence failure, however, is unprecedented and
demands a better solution. Many innocent victims do not understand why their families are killed. Wars are messy; bombs
explode in the wrong place, killing many fathers, mothers,
and children.

Right now, too many countries hate our guts. Some may
call themselves our allies but deep inside, even they despise
us. We do not want this animosity to grow, and we need to
work to regain the trust and friendship of our fellow countries

through diplomacy and peaceful negotiations. We need to choose war only as a last resort.

We went into Iraq and Afghanistan, and spent trillions of dollars that resulted in many casualties, both military and civilian. We did so because of the attack on the Twin Towers in New York. Four thousand people died in that attack, which was the largest act of terrorism the United States had ever witnessed on its own land. We finally did kill Bin Laden, the principal mastermind. We also nabbed and killed Saddam Hussein. Both of these men committed terrible atrocities against their own people, and ours. But the price paid for these two deaths was very high: trillions of dollars and countless lives lost. Now it looks as though we are in a state of endless war. No timeline for ending the war in Afghanistan exists, and it is hard to comprehend whether or not we have made any significant gains by winning the war in Iraq. It does not matter if we have the most powerful war equipment in the world; the new wars are different from the old ones, and even more dangerous. The bottom line is that we spent trillions, and have very little to show for it—at least, very little the average person can see.

These two wars have been the longest and costliest in American history. We are borrowing too much money from the Chinese, putting future generations at risk for an unnecessary recession. We need cuts in war spending. We need to use our resources for strategic defense, and invest in cybersecurity, robotics, and technology to help us win and end the war. We also need to exhaust all diplomatic means before even contemplating going to war. Right now, other countries—like China, India, Japan, Korea, Brazil, and others—are investing in their country's infrastructure while we whittle away our money on wars.

By not investing in our own schools, industries, and technology, we are falling behind other countries and have to continue borrowing money because we are no longer competitive. If we continue in this matter, the whole country will be bankrupt. We need to change our way of doing things. The federal government has the power to fix the niggling problems faced by the nation, and I propose several options.

Right now, nearly 20 million Americans are out of work. Nine trillion dollars of household income has vanished like magic. The deficit is nearly $1 trillion a year. Two million construction jobs have been cut from the payrolls of companies that are bankrupt or working at minimum capacity. Can you imagine what $2 billion a week would do for small businesses? Why do we go to war if the benefits are so minimal, and what we really want is economic prosperity?

An old adage says, "If you want peace, you need to be prepared for war." We are—and have been—prepared for so long. We have the best military in the world. No nation has the military capabilities of America, but we need to consider new wars could be more catastrophic than those in the past, given our new technologies. Weapons need to be removed from the equation. The fast pace of the new generation is part of the problem. Since the 1990s, in just over 100 years, the world has changed faster than in the past two thousand. Improvements to electricity, telephones, running water, airplanes, televisions, indoor plumbing, computers, and more have skyrocketed. In just 100 years, the industrial and technological revolutions have transformed the face of the world.

It is the most important era since the beginning of civilization, with the United States planted firmly in the center.

This comes, however, at a price. A rapid rate of change is not free, and the United States, having been at the forefront of this transformation, now must pay. Environmental concerns, conflicts with other countries, generational problems, economic crises, the vulnerability of our borders north and south, and uncertainty of the future all drain our resources.

One of our biggest fears is that the violence spreading throughout Latin America will pass through our porous borders and create a very dangerous situation. When I came to America, I thought the police, sheriffs, immigration officers, highway patrol, DEA officers, the FBI, and the CIA were honest. I believed them incorruptible, unlike the law enforcement officers in Mexico. Through the years, however, I have been met with a rude surprise. I have seen the newscasts flashing the arrests of many agents at different ranks in the law. These incidents have shaken my trust in these officers. Nevertheless, I am glad to say not all are bad. I believe, like in everything else, a few bad apples destroy things; in this case, the few corrupt officials dented the integrity of the majority.

In the last few years alone, almost 150 immigration officers have been found guilty of corruption. It is essential that our government do something about this to protect those vulnerable crossings. Because of the recession, the influx of immigrants has been decreasing, but the real threat to our national security is that terrorists may cross the River, or the violence in Mexico may cross the border. This presents a huge problem for our authorities as well as our general population. Just imagine, in one small Mexican city soldiers found more than 150 corpses in a couple of mass graves. That can scare even those who like to see scary movies. More mass graves can be found in other Mexican states, not to mention the casualties of drug wars littering the streets. Mexico is truly a war zone.

We must protect our borders against the delinquency, and against the drug war being fought between the governments and the cartels. Of course, the U.S. government should identify and deport people responsible for crimes. But those people differ from those of us who came to this country to work and prosper, to pursue the American Dream. I ask the government to recognize the difference, and not harass and deport the hard-working people who come here to better their lives.

This country boasts a strong military—but we are burdened by a weak economy. The threat of yet another war with Iran is very real, which makes negotiations between the two even more critical. God help us all if negotiations fail while the military option remains on the table.

I have identified five societal problems that will never completely go away, no matter how much money we put into resolving them:

1. Drug Addiction. With education and awareness programs, this epidemic can be contained but not eliminated.

2. Prostitution. As the oldest profession in the world, it will never fully disappear.

3. Wars. Wars have been fought since the beginning of time, but too many are happening right now.

4. Terrorism. Terrorists have existed for thousands of years. While terrorism can be diminished, it cannot be stopped, as it is a sign people are struggling.

5. Destruction of the planet—and ourselves. Shutting down all the nuclear plants in the world will not stop us from destroying ourselves and our planet. Too many toxic chemicals that can put future generations at stake surround us. Plus, where will we put all the nuclear waste? I do not think there will be enough sites to fill to protect people and the environment. Look at Chernobyl and the recent nuclear disaster in Japan. This pales in comparison to what could happen in a densely populated area, where millions of people could lose their lives. That is what I mean when I say danger exists in every country that plays with this harmful technology.

The Afghanistan war is unwinnable because of the opium that is involved, and we already know drug wars cannot be won. We know wars on terror wars cannot be won either, and we are fighting Al Qaeda and the Taliban—two partners in terror. No matter what generals at the Pentagon have said, we are not going to win this war. The Afghan people have been at war for several centuries, and will not stand for us to win. So, we need to get out of there at the earliest opportunity.

The military machine in the United States is massive and complex, which sooner rather than later will have serious consequences in the economy. It may be counterintuitive but in this era, more spending on defense does not result in sounder economic growth. Greater defense spending likely benefits military contractors, but certainly not the rest of the American population.

We need to understand the catastrophic impact of these prolonged wars on the next generation of Americans. Do we want our children using machine guns as early 10 years old? This is where we are headed, if we do not change our direction of defense policy—from being a war-prone nation to becoming one with a super defense system.

Now our military is giving a green light for women to be part of the front-line combat force. Are they aware of the collateral damage of this decision? The impact of this on the children of these women soldiers would be devastating; they would grow up in trauma, living under the constant fear of losing their mothers on the battlefield, or imagining their parent to return home with lost limbs and incapacitated. I know we do not have as many soldiers in the military as compared to China or North Korea; but these days defense is all about weapon and defense power, and not the capacity of the military force.

In that regard, we are far ahead of our enemy nation, thus eliminating the need for women to join the Armed Forces. We are not waging a war, and I hope there is a slim possibility of one in the near future. Therefore, it is not in the best interest of the nation to have women who are also mothers get killed in the front line. We have everything required to defend our nation, so why not send robots to the front line? This way, even if we lose the war, we lose only robots and money. On the other hand, when we send our people to such senseless wars, the extent of damage to precious life is insurmountable— even if we win. Avoiding war is far better for America's future and the future of its citizens, especially the children. It is not recommended that any country go to war, but those who do fail to grasp the horrid consequences of war, which includes the depletion—if not outright elimination—of its own assets.

Some countries in the world seek large-scale nuclear power in the form of arms and ammunition. Such countries do not seem to have learned anything from the Chernobyl incident or the catastrophic nuclear explosions in Japan. These countries may get away with ignoring past disasters or terrors, but they will not escape the consequences.

In Chernobyl, the radiation from a leaking reactor was enough to destroy an area larger than the size of a whole city in the United States. Whether this was due to lack of proper maintenance or negligence on the part of plant authorities, we can look at Chernobyl as an example of how much damage can be done from seeking nuclear weapons. Even in the United States, with all the high-level security and maintenance, we have occasionally come close to a disaster situation in one of our nuclear power plants. Just imagine nuclear weaponry being handled by countries with far less effective maintenance systems.

As a well-prepared and equipped nation, we must know where we need to invest our money—whether on education, healthcare, rebuilding our infrastructure, replenishing our spiritual wellbeing, or waging wars. Other nations of the world know of the military might of the United States of America. We need to use our might with caution, and for our own cultural, societal, and economic benefit.

Every other country in this world knows us as a military superpower. We do not need to stage a war just because some dictator or tyrant criticizes us. The tyrant criticizes us purposefully to provoke and engage us in a war. Mere provocation does not justify declaring war.

Wars are like sports contests; the less the athlete speaks before the match, the more efficiently he can perform in the fight. If he wins, then it is excellent; but, if he loses, at least he did not say anything before the fight, and can say anything he wants after the match is over. It is exactly the same with wars. We should not want new wars. Have we not had enough suicides of returning veterans and the broken families left behind? At least 22 veterans kill themselves on a daily basis. Multiply that over five years and we will have 40,000 soldier deaths from self-inflicted destruction and without any military confrontation. Now imagine those women with children committing suicide; for those innocent human beings, the damage is irreparable and will be carried through several generations to come. It is sad our government is not able to visualize the imminent effects of allowing women in combat.

The danger of new-age sophisticated weapons that a few governments are trying to pile up is a growing concern for all countries of the world, as these weapons pose a serious threat to the environment and mankind. Chernobyl is a glaring example of the hazards of a nuclear plant not safely maintained.

Just imagine the risks to the world if a country possesses 100 nuclear bombs that then get blown up by enemy bombs. This could cause unimaginable disaster for the world.

The dangers of present-day wars are that those nations using biological weapons and nuclear arms will cause devastation to other countries and destroy millions of lives. These weapons can ignite at any time, any day, in areas of the world that have been at war for thousands of years. Why does a country start nuclear warfare knowing it will also be affected in the process?

Despite whatever aversions we may have toward war, we must be grateful to all those soldiers and veterans who have fought and continue to fight the wars, risking their lives to protect the country and its people. No one can grasp the horrors encountered by these courageous men and women. No one except these soldiers knows the pain they endured in captivity. We can never forget the ones who did not return to their families; and we can never forget those who come back with unspeakable injuries forever etched on their hearts. Some soldiers return without physical injuries, but they silently suffer from the psychological trauma they went through. Our heart goes out to every one of these heroic soldiers.

The Syrian confrontation was too close for comfort. This time, the diplomacy worked well, but we were just one decision away from confrontation. Iran looks like it is willing, hopefully, to negotiate—and that is a chance to open the door to diplomacy to work one more time.

There are too many wars, too many women on the front lines, too many violent movies, and too many addictive computer games. If we add the social Web, all this combined creates a time bomb that will explode and damage too many children of the new generations to come.

Our government needs to make smart decisions about the military, economy, education, infrastructure, and immigration. They must, with good planning and action, make the best solution for the new generations. Right now, the government looks like they are on a collision course if nothing is done to minimize the big mess we are in right now, which is growing like a huge wildfire—too fast, too soon, and too unpredictable for all the American children who are the most vulnerable to society's problems.

CHAPTER III

THE IMMIGRATION SOLUTION

Ilegal immmigrants are an important work force in America, but we need them legal.

S. G.

Many people in America hate immigrants, all for different reasons. Some think they are a bunch of criminals. Some think they are gang members or drug addicts. Others are afraid immigrants have come to steal their jobs. The list goes on. The truth is we are, for the most part, all immigrants. The only original Americans are Native Americans, who interestingly are far less complaining than the rest of Americans who belong to families of immigrants. Why bother to complain if almost all the people who live in America are from immigrant descent? We are represented by more than 150 countries; whether we like it or not, this is the reality of America. This is the way our nation has been; where we are now is because of those first waves of immigrants who came here and built this great nation, and who are still coming—maybe in smaller numbers, but they will continue arriving. It is not going to stop anytime soon.

Some may think it is bad for the country to have people of different nationalities, but the strength of America is the diversity of its people. Consider these examples: Albert Einstein, the Nobel Prize winner in physics who discovered the Theory of Relativity and was one of the first to reconcile the laws of Electromagnetic Fields and the laws of Mechanics, was born in Germany. John F. Kennedy was born in Massachusetts, but his great-grandfather emigrated from Ireland.

Thomas Edison, considered the greatest inventor of all time, was of English descent. Guillermo Gonzalez Cameraena is the Mexican engineer who invented the color television. Nikola Tesla, a Serbian American inventor, is regarded as one of the greatest electrical engineers in the United States. The computer tycoon, Michael Dell, was born in Houston, to Jewish descendants. He started building computers and shipping them out of his dorm room, and became the world's largest PC-maker. The latest inventor of the high-tech era and the premium Apple brand, Steve Jobs, was the son of a Syrian entrepreneur.

Immigrants are the heart and soul of this nation, and we can cite many more examples of great immigrant achievers. These are the ones who accomplished the American Dream; some are still living and enjoying the rewards. Believing illegal immigration threatens our national security is illegal immigration is a fallacy. If, in their home countries, such people live and work in penurious conditions, they will find a way to come to the Promised Land. They will come by foot or by car, by plane, by sea or by the desert. Some will have visas; others will pay large sums of cash to smugglers. But, they will come, sooner rather than later, and the more our economy improves the greater the influx of immigrants. Immigrants have moved here from all over the world; this has been the trend. Perhaps one day another country will represent the ideal life; but, for now, the country with the greatest opportunities in the world is right here—America. Like it or not, immigrants will populate this vast nation. The problem is when an economic recession causes people to blame illegal immigration for all the problems with healthcare, education, and employment opportunities. While it is understandable to think that way, we cannot forget the benefits our economy reaps through immigrant labor in agriculture, construction, and the so-called "dirty" jobs.

The global economic crisis, not illegal workers, is responsible for the bad shape of the American economy. Illegal immigrants represent our most vulnerable people, the ones who have neither a voice nor a vote. They have nothing to do with the crisis. Furthermore, immigrants are the ones who have been doing all the hard work lately. First, it was slaves; now, it is immigrants. You may say immigrants are unintelligent and only good for slog work, but in 2009 one-third of America's doctoral degrees went to students from immigrant families.

You claim you can work in laborious and industrious situation, but only a few of you have the persistence to do that. You also claim you can work in a 50- or 100-story building construction site, but only a few of you can risk your lives that way. You say you can work on a scorching 140-degree road-paving job that almost toasts your face every day; again I say only a few of you can do that. You say you can even work in the fields, picking fruit or harvesting some other crop; and a few can do that.

Can you paint bridges amid the toxicity of industrial paints, knowing that, even if you make good money, your life expectancy is diminished because even protective gear cannot prevent you from inhaling dangerous chemicals? Not many can say, "I can do that." The list is too long for this book; and even if a few could do it, we need millions of people to restart our economy's engine. This is why I propose we prioritize the immigration solution. If 20 million Americans respond "yes" to the following 20 questions, we would not need illegal immigrants.

1. If you like to work with demolition hammers six days a week, eight hours a day, we do not need illegal immigrants.

2. If you like to work on highways in temperatures higher than 120 degrees, we do not need illegal immigrants.

3. If you like to work digging trenches every day with your own hands, we do not need illegal immigrants.

4. If you like to lay brick or rock in houses, we do not need illegal immigrants.

5. If you like to work on concrete driveways, foundations, and floors with your hands, in harsh temperatures, we do not need illegal immigrants.

6. If you like to work in city landfills in inclement weather year-round, with the never-ending stench of garbage, we do not need illegal immigrants.

7. If you like to work under the basements of old houses, knowing that at any moment a snake or spider can bite you or 10,000 bees can sting you, we do not need illegal immigrants.

8. If you think you can work eight-hour shifts, seven days a week, in inclement weather in the fields, we do not need illegal immigrants.

9. If you think you can cook all kinds of food, and work seven days a week preparing food or cleaning dishes in a restaurant, we do not need illegal immigrants.

10. If you think you can be on the roof of a three-story apartment building, putting shingles under a scorching sun with no protection, we do not need illegal immigrants.

11. If you think you can deal with old people in nursing homes, six days a week, eight days a week, we do not need illegal immigrants.

12. If you are willing to work in a small metal-fabrication factory as a welder, knowing you will probably lose most of your vision in 10 or 20 years, we do not need illegal immigrants.

13. If you like to paint houses with airless sprayers, knowing your lifespan will be shorter, we do not need illegal immigrants.

14. If you are not afraid to work in a 30-, 50-, or 100-story building, we do not need illegal immigrants.

15. If you like to work with a pick and shovel all day, we do not need illegal immigrants.

16. If you are willing to work for minimum wage as a hotel housekeeper, we do not need illegal immigrants.

17. If you are willing as parents to have 20 children in your family, we do not need illegal immigrants.

18. If you are willing to work on concrete bridges, some as high as 100 feet tall, we do not need illegal immigrants.

19. If you like to work in the garden every day, you are not allergic to cedar, poison ivy, or poison oak; we do not need illegal immigrants.

20. If you want India, China, Korea, Japan, or other countries to become number one in economic power, with the United States trailing behind, we do not need illegal immigrants.

Yes ___No

If your answer is "yes" to all the questions, then we do not need illegal immigrants—but only if 20 million Americans say "yes" and choose to work in every single one of these jobs. Otherwise, we need illegal immigrants. Our task then becomes to legalize them before we put them to work.

If you are of Italian descent, your grandparents encountered discrimination in the 1920s, when they came to the United States. If you are of Irish descent, your ancestors were not welcomed here. American history is rife with protests against immigration. Sometimes such protests were minimal, but they always existed—and these days are no exception. We are facing racism because of bad economic times. We are seeing lately a deep problem of hate against defenseless illegal immigrants that has nothing to do with the economic crisis. The real responsibility lies in the wars, the oriental manufacturing competency, the OPEC high oil prices, the speculators in New York, and the monopolies of American gas stations charging astronomical rates for gasoline.

The government has been asleep for so many years in many areas of this country's infrastructure. We do not have bullet trains, superhighways, or super dams. What if the government sends our 15 million illegal immigrants back to their countries of origin, if that were possible? But, I know that it is almost impossible—and what about the global competence of Japan, China, Korea, India and Brazil? With what labor force will we compete with those countries?

We need those 15 million people, but we do not need illegal immigrants. We need immigrants with legal papers. We need people willing to work in factories, agriculture fields, nursing homes, on construction sites, cleaning houses and hotels, and so on—but with papers. We need to legalize illegal immigrants quickly, and give them full protection of the law. Even if a few people can work any hard-labor job—and I am sure several thousand people can—we need millions of people in order to get out of this global competition crisis. A few people will not do any good.

Take the following example. Imagine two, labor-intensive factories, one in China and the other in the United States, manufacturing the same product. The Chinese factory uses cheap labor, abundant in the country, while the American company uses cheap—but illegal—labor. If the INS rids the whole American factory of illegal workers, leaving the factory without daily wageworkers because the American people do not like to work in a harsh work environment, who wins? Not the government, not the American people, and especially not the now-empty factory. The real winner is the Chinese factory that now has no competition from the United States, and it is too bad for the town where this factory was once a direct or indirect source of jobs. If this factory had created 1,000 jobs, then at least 20,000 American people would be making a living from it.

Yet the government, instead of addressing the immigration problem, opts for the easy solution: deport the illegal workers and pay no mind to the consequences. If the government chose the best solution, legalizing the illegal immigrants, we will have enough hands to compete against those countries currently surpassing us in economic growth and prosperity. If, however, the government ignores this nation's best interests, the economic crisis will continue because the real problems will remain unresolved. In several months, immigration agents raided nearly 7000 businesses that were using illegal workers, killing a good part of the economic recovery. We are talking about billions of dollars lost, and guess where those jobs reappeared—in Asia.

When I was a child in 1960, my mother owned a grocery store on the Mexican side of the border, just two blocks from where Cuidad Acuna, Mexico, bordered Del Rio, Texas. Every other day, we saw lines of men going to the River, sometimes five or ten men coming from States south of Mexico and trying to pass through the borders of the Rio Bravo. Several of our neighbors were dedicated to passing the immigrants through the River. It was very dangerous; at that time many people drowned trying to cross those treacherous waters. Our store was the last chance for those people to buy groceries for the long journey ahead. Some only walked for minutes, some walked for hours, and a few walked for days until they crossed to a safe ranch or city; it all depended on the guide.

The Border Patrol was very soft. The United States needed plenty of workers to work in extreme and dirty jobs, and Mexico was supplying the demand. Almost no one complained, on either side of the border. The police in Mexico never bothered the people who were trying to cross the River to try to prosper in the Land of Opportunity. The Border Patrol team was so small in number that Texas was unable to stop even 10% of those crossing illegally—some of who even crossed the border several times without getting caught.

As time passed, the Border Patrol began to hire more personnel and the easy passes disappeared. Instead of crossing a few yards from the main bridge, immigrants started to go a few miles on either side of the bridge. Now, they frequently go into the wild to get through. Also, as time passed, we started seeing people from far south in Mexico; in the 1980s, we started seeing many people from South America crossing in large numbers. The American government gave those arriving from South America papers to stay in this country. The illegal immigrants are still crossing the River, but in smaller numbers lately; and not just because the Border Patrol has increased in size, but also because the economy is in a slump with few opportunities to find jobs. Latin Americans come to the United States with the intention to go straight to work, not to sit idly by; they can do better than that in their countries of origin.

In the 1960s, relations between Mexico and the United States were so good that, during a celebration of the Mexican Revolution, on the 20th of November, in Cuidad Acuna, Mexico, there was a parade where the Mexican paraders went to the

American side, in Del Rio, Texas, to perform—without any papers whatsoever. The bridge was open to anyone who wanted to cross to see his or her family or neighbors in the other country. At the same time, American paraders performed on the Mexican side. It was called the Parade of a Good Neighbor. One of my greatest memories is the high school band music, the Shriners, and Adelita—the ex-wife of Pancho Villa, in a 1927 car. (Pancho Villa was considered a villain in the United States, but a revolutionary hero in Mexico.)

Mexico and America were building one of the biggest dams in the world at the time, in the Rio Bravo, between Del Rio, Texas and Ciudad Acuna, Mexico. Everything was based on mutual help between these neighboring countries. I do not know if there were "papers checks" in other ports of entry, but there certainly were no checks between the two cities that day. The American economy was booming. They did not have immigration checkpoints outside of Del Rio or Eagle Pass, Texas, whether in 50, 75, or any other number of miles. Those without papers would wait until the free day at the bridge checkpoint; they would come to work for several years in any state. Every city was booming and generating job opportunities everywhere. No one asked if you were from China, Latin America, or Africa; they just asked if you wanted to work.

In the 1960s and 1970s, there was no apparent racism, because there was work for anyone who wanted to work. All of the major cities were building their infrastructures. The construction of new buildings and houses was a nonstop enterprise. On November 20, 1984, I went to North Carolina. I do not remember which city I was in, but one thing I remember was a sign on the entrance of a famous restaurant. The sign read, "No Blacks allowed in this place."

Can you imagine? It was 1984, and still segregation was accepted in North Carolina. What a shame. These days, we are talking about our struggling economy and the scarcity of jobs; whom do we blame now? Many say undocumented immigrants are at fault, primarily Latinos. The real fault, however, lies within. America is devastated by foreign competition, and too many American people buy items made outside America. The debt of our government has America on her knees.

Illegal immigrants work very hard every day to pump up the economy, and to help us emerge from the crisis. If the economy picks up, it will be good for everybody in the long run; only hard work and smart decisions by our government will bring about an economic recovery. In the meantime, illegal immigrants are helping to improve the pace of growth and recovery. As soon as this happens, there will be jobs for everyone in America, and opportunities for companies and workers to improve their income in the foreseeable future. We can all pull the wagon, together with temporary workers, to improve the productive sectors of an ailing and battered economy.

To recapitulate some of the adventures of those brave men and women who risked their lives to come to this country of opportunities, sometimes from nations far away, would take thousands of books because every illegal immigrant has a story to tell. Many of these heroes did not live to tell their story; some drowned in the River, some died in the desert, and some became victims of crime in Mexico. This nation's demand for illegal immigrants is not going to stop anytime soon—as long as agriculture, construction, and hard and dirty work needs to be done. The illegal crossings will continue for years, because the problem has become so complex that there is no easy solution.

We need to deal with this immigration problem sooner or later; the sooner we confront this issue, the better it will be for America. Some state immigration laws stigmatize Hispanic illegal immigrants—just because of their racial appearance. It is easy for state legislatures to implement reforms that do not work. States pass laws that allow arrests of innocent people whose only crime is working hard in an honest way for the benefit of this great nation. To add to their woes, the children of the illegal immigrants who are in schools and colleges around the nation await the Dream Act that is not coming, even after all the time invested trying to make it happen. If our prime competitors in the world are well educated, but we do not graduate immigrant students, it is *hara kiri*. Several thousand students, born to illegal immigrants but U.S. citizens are prevented from fulfilling their dream of graduating from college and serving their country in their chosen profession. If these people are as legitimate as any American citizen, why do states insist on putting the brakes on the prosperity of the nation? Some state legislatures are rushing to impose immigration laws, others bar illegal immigrants from public colleges for the so-called benefit of the United States. They are wrong.

State and local governments should instead work together to solve the problem that affects our entire nation. Some states require businesses to check the legal status of their employees. Some, like Mississippi, have enacted laws where working in the State is illegal; it is punishable with felony charges. Other states penalize landlords for renting to illegal immigrants. It is easy to impose strict immigration laws, but what about fixing the immigration problem? That sounds a little more complicated; yet not too many state legislatures want to submit plans to solve the problem because it is easier to blame the economic crisis on illegal immigrants.

Economists, however, know that the nation's economic crisis has nothing to do with illegal immigrants. Illegal immigrants have nothing to do with the wars we still fight; they have nothing to do with major American companies that relocated overseas. These state laws, like the ones in the Carolinas, are becoming harsher; they are like the Black Codes of the 1800s. We are in 2014. These laws have been created to induce fear among the Hispanic community. The Black Codes were laws enacted to deal with the Black community in the 19th century.

Some states say illegal immigrants cost taxpayers large sums of money, but they have not investigated the amount of money contributed by that labor force, whether directly or indirectly. They do not want to see or publish these figures; if they do, they will see that immigrants are the only ones willing to work in laborious and necessary jobs. An illegal immigrant crackdown will impact the harvest. Imagine what a widespread immigration crackdown could cause to America. Yes, you know, America could collapse without illegal workers, period. Several states that are not so harsh against illegal immigrants, like California, Illinois, Texas, Washington, and Connecticut. Perhaps that is because these states recognize the tremendous value of immigrant laborers.

Immigrants are not the only targets of discrimination; some states still discriminate against U.S. citizens because of their race and ethnicity. But, we are also from more than 150 countries. The bad economy is raising the tide of racism in a few states; this is a disgrace to America—and to the people who live within its borders. To balance and unify people from 150 nations is not an easy task. This task, however, has never been easy; it has been like this for the past 100 years, and will continue to be so.

If you think you own this nation, let me tell you that this nation belongs to everybody who lives and works in this nation. It does not matter how many people have other national ties; what matters is that they are legal. Instead of constructive ideas and solutions for their state's economy, some state legislators only have destructive laws when it comes to immigration solutions. They are only damaging their country's economic sector in their states, because they do not recognize the contributions of the illegal immigrants. They are blind to accepting the benefits of the immigrants to the U.S. economy.

What these legislators are trained to do is over forty years old. It does not matter how the economy is doing; for years now the American people have not wanted to do hard labor. The American people prefer to relegate the hard work to somebody else; and these days, "somebody else" is the illegal immigrant. I do not blame the American people if they can make a good amount of money in a business, in the stock market, in the Internet. Why do they need to work hard? Some American people and some legislators think the undocumented people are taking the lunch from the hands of Americans; I believe, however, that those responsible for taking the lunch away from both U.S. citizens and immigrants are the Asian people. The Chinese are the main ones; but some politicians try to blame the innocents, the most fragile. They want to inculpate the immigrants responsible for the weak economy.

For a long time, America has been growing animosity against other races, which is understandable; because, in the United States, there are people from more than 150 nations living on American soil. Some of these do not like each other, which gets worse when the economy is slow, and the racists play the blame game. Yet for immigrants, legal or illegal, when we cross the River or arrive by boat or plane, we develop an instant triumphant feeling of confidence in success, that people of all nationalities are capable of living the American Dream.

Some do not try hard enough, or do not make it for different reasons, but they know that, in America, there will always be better working conditions than in their country of origin. Most of them try their best; and in most cases, people find success in different areas of life: economics, sports, spirituality, and so on. We know the United States lacks a good immigration system, and that our government is working to solve one of the oldest problems our nation has been facing for decades. For example, if the government takes the extreme negative position of sending every undocumented person back home, and thinks it is a good idea to deport 10 or 15 million people, who is going to back up the labor force to beat the global competition? I believe we can get over this by joining together, instead of separating ourselves. What matters is they are here, right now, ready to help this great nation return to its former glory.

States immigration laws do not provide for long-term solutions for the millions of immigrants. This presents a serious threat to the economy and the productivity of our country; if we do not fix the problem, the food will not show up on our tables because people will not work in the agriculture fields to produce fruits and vegetables. No immigrants mean less food for everyone else. Besides, who is going to compete with the 1.3 billion Chinese in manufacturing? The only chance we have to compete with the Chinese is with a strong labor force, and this human resource requirement can be fulfilled through illegal immigrants. Immigrants, once more, are ready to take any manufacturing job that will be made available in the near future.

Enacting anti-immigration laws may look good in newspapers or on TV, but that will not solve the general problem. It will, for sure, disrupt businesses in those states with these laws. It will endanger farms across the nation; if the government clears the fields of illegal immigrants, do you seriously think that American citizens are going to work in this inclement weather, 12 hours a day? You are kidding me. The last time the American people worked on a farm was around the 1940s and 1960s. If a farm needs, say, 200 workers, how many U.S. citizens will show up for those positions? If the farm owner is lucky, 10 at the most will turn up; and 90% of the produce will be lost. No hands available to pick those agricultural products mean no fruits or vegetables on your table.

The people of this great nation are mainly made up of immigrants, or relatives of immigrants. They came to the United States from every corner of the planet. America has millions of talented immigrants who, at one time, were illegal immigrants. We cannot stop the influx of immigrants, but we need to offer a workable solution for this country's future. The enactment of immigration reforms affects the economic situation of the whole nation. I know, for a fact, that a "no illegal immigrants" policy would result in austerity, recession, and even depression. If immigrants receive temporary worker papers, they can apply for jobs, buy cars, open bank accounts, pay taxes, and much more. The illegal immigrants are intelligent and capable of performing any high-skill job. Many are capable of doing any high-tech job.

All of this will be offered after the economy starts to boom, and the American people are employed. Consequently, we can start with the temporary workers until the reform is passed. Some people have doubts about immigrants' technological potential. Of course, they have plenty of that to offer, because immigrants are the backbone of America's success as a world power. Hard-working immigrants only create opportunities to improve our economy. Both Republicans and Democrats need to understand the value of immigrant workers—their contribution to the economy and our infrastructure. Immigrants have helped and will continue to help build a better America. To solve the immigration problem, the United States has three options.

1.   A good option is to act fast to solve the problem right now, and start the process of immigration reform.

2.   A bad option is for the government to wait too long to make a decision.

3.   The worst option is if the government continues to do nothing at all.

I have provided enough reasons to convince the government to speed up at least temporary workers' papers so that they can work then work on reform and other necessary solutions to the benefit of this great nation. The clock is ticking; the sooner they solve the problem, the less the economy will suffer. We need solutions now, not tomorrow, because tomorrow may be too late.

Some state legislatures are rushing to impose immigration laws. Some states bar illegal immigrants from public colleges; they think it is for the benefit of the country, but they are totally unjustified and short-ranged. Instead, legislators should work together to solve the problem that affects not only their own state but also the nation as a whole. I do not want reforms made today or legislation to be rushed, or to make mistakes in the process. What I believe can work for both the United States and the illegal immigrants living within its borders, is to go to their lawyers and get a simple temporary working resident paper. This would cost about $2,000, and would provide the opportunity to live and work anyplace in the country. They should pay their taxes until the best reform bill is passed; that way, the government will have control of immigrant numbers, taxes, where they live, and what they do. Those with criminal records will not be entitled to a paper unless a lawyer presents a case, and that would need a separate proceeding.

The human talent is already available here, ready, and willing to help us get out of this economic mess; we just need to work on the immigration laws. Immigrants are ready for change; they are waiting for a green light, and will accept any kind of immigration reform so that they, too, can contribute to the rebuilding of the economy. They are willing to pay any amount of money the government desires, but the decision needs to be made now. If we continue as we have for the past 12 years, nothing will happen. We cannot afford to wait.

The necessity is mutual; undocumented immigrants need papers, and America needs a good, solid labor force to counter the tough challenges we face. If this is done right, it will be a victory for America. We have two choices. Either we legalize the 15 million illegal immigrants and put them to work, or we continue to do nothing and wait until it is too late. Other nations will have better economies, while the United States will still be in crisis. This seems difficult, but it can create a solution to a problem that has needed attention for too long. It is time for Congress to make this a priority, and make America proud of our elected representatives. For once it is time we be remembered for being united.

This is your chance, Mr. President, to show your nation what you are capable of doing with the right decisions. Why wait until we are second, if we can continue to be the Number One producer of goods in the world? The decision needs to be made now, not tomorrow, because that could be too late. This process of working papers could be as simple as obtaining a driver's license; you are halfway there. The other half is to conduct yourself well, pay your taxes, and work for several years until full reform is passed. These taxes workers pay will provide additional funds for other job creation programs.

I know this proposal will be greeted with antagonism, but I believe this will make our nation stronger by providing papers and allowing illegal immigrants to learn English, go to school, gain new skills, and more. The immigrants who live here should have the same rights as the Cubans: to stay as soon as they step onto American soil. We need legal papers, not segregation, hate, or civil rights violations. The illegal immigrants live in constant fear. We do not need to befriend them, but to deport students is not wise. We must foresee the benefit they will be to our country when they finish college. We need 20 million skilled workers, just to keep up with our European and Asian competitors. We need all the Latin American people who want to come and work, because the population of China is the equivalent of North America and South America, combined. We need those people to work in agriculture, just to keep up with the demand for food. If we do not keep these people working for American companies, we will be in trouble.

On top of our other problems, we have climate change. We have serious destabilization of our food supply, and prices could go sky-high. If you want to pay $10 to $20 for one apple, we do not need illegal workers. If you want to pay $500,000 for a house worth $100,000, then we do not need illegal workers. We are foolish to assume the American economy will improve if we send all the illegal immigrants home. I believe that America, without those 15 million immigrants, would have a devastating impact on our economy, starting with agricultural fields and ending with, manufacturing and construction until our entire infrastructure is engulfed.

I know the logistics of issuing papers to 15 million unauthorized immigrants overnight may seem insurmountable. Yet I also know this paperwork process can be accomplished on short notice by deploying several lawyers with time to offer.

Every day, thousands of people from all over the world try to enter the United States, but only a few succeed. Our borders, therefore, need to be more secure; to prevent the infiltration of crime taints our land. Security is inevitable for all our frontiers bordering Mexico and Canada. Public safety is a priority for every person who aspires to live and work with integrity in America. No exceptions should be made when it comes to security and the safety of our people.

We need to stop wasting time prosecuting these honest, diligent workers, who came to this country in hopes of improving the lives of their families suffering in their home countries. Let us go and give the papers to these people, and dry their tears. We need to expedite the action to be taken to grant legal papers to every such immigrant living in the United States right now. If they are able to pass police and background checks, then, without further ado, and avoiding red tape, the immigration reform should be decided on who should be granted permanent citizenship and who should be give temporary status with no benefits.

I do not know if Congress will be willing to give temporary work authorization papers to undocumented immigrants. If they do, they first need to factor in critical data before approving any immigration reform. Congress needs to know:

1. The exact number of immigrants currently in the United States;

2. The age of immigrants living in America on the date of application;

3. Immigrants' marital status, place and type of occupation, education background, length of stay in the

country, immigration status, employment status, disability status, criminal background, taxpaying status;

4.   How to obtain the fingerprints of millions of undocumented people;

5.   How many would like to go to school; how many people are from foreign countries; their current address; and

6.   How many have criminal histories, and might need a lawyer to help prepare them to become eligible for papers.

If the government gives the illegal immigrant temporary papers, the government should also require that, in order to get a temporary visa, the illegal person must formally agree, from that day forward, to buy only American-made products. The 11 or 15 million illegal immigrants, in order to qualify for resident papers after immigration reform is passed, will need to present plenty of invoices for purchases of American-made products.

Stores will be required to put "Made in America" on the invoices. Can you imagine? The buying power of 15 million people will be enough to restart our manufacturing engine; if the rest of Americans follow, we will no longer fear our Chinese competitors. Immigration reform should include a plan to expedite the entrance of visitors south of the border. It is a matter of planning and decision, without compromising security, because that is our first concern. Yet, putting

border checkpoints at the main cities that see the most visitors per year, like Laredo, Texas, is inefficient and uneconomi-
cal. People who travel by bus 10 or 15 hours from south of
the border should not have to wait in line six to nine hours
to cross the bridge. But if there is one agent with one dog, we
should put in three agents with three dogs, or four and four. If
there is only one x-ray machine, install two or three more, and
so on. If there is no more space, take the bus to another place
for inspection. Something needs to be done, because thousands of people lose an entire day's work in just the last mile
of bumper-to-bumper traffic moving. Can you imagine how
many thousands of people a day cross all the major borders?
We laud ourselves on our vast technical capabilities, but you
would never know that by looking at our borders.

After the government controls the number of immigrants,
their ages and origins, the ways they enter the United States,
and the type of work they will be able to do, the background
police can check where they live, where they work, and how
many times they have entered this country. They can identify
those who are labeled safe and those who pose a risk for security; who will be a candidate for permanent residence, and
who is a "temporary papers only" candidate; those who will be
working in a technical position and those who will be working in the fields or whether we even need to give temporary
visas for that type of employment; and who can pay for temporary papers and who cannot. We can learn the most vulnerable points of entry by recording how each immigrant entered
the country, and then our government will find out how to
counter those weak checkpoints. There are so many things our
government can learn from those 15 million people—after

they give them temporary papers, they can use all the valuable information they can discern from all those immigrants in order to write the best immigration reform our legislators can.

With all the numbers, the facts, the areas that need reinforcement, and money this will generate, we should be more accurate when making good immigration reform. It is time for decisions, and immigration is no exception. But, it is better to give temporary papers to all immigrants who live in the United States right now, and wait to create the best immigration reform ever implemented by this country. If we wait, we are more likely to develop a real and permanent solution to the immigration problem for future generations. If the government can grant an opportunity for every temporary immigrant to leave the country and return to their country of origin at least once a year, it would be a big plus to future legal immigrants. By visiting their relatives, they will recharge the batteries of the American dream.

If the U.S. government has the fingerprints and computers for control, it is only a matter of having a few more personnel at the checkpoints and one or two lines for those with temporary papers to enter the United States. Imagine the economic boom every State on the border of the United States and Mexico will experience, not to mention a boom in airline reservations and all types of transportation.

If the U.S. government does not legalize the immigrants, who is going to continue to do the work America needs to prosper? In two decades, 78 million people will be retired and collecting billions of dollars every year. What will our government do right now, if it already has budget trouble? Yes, in 20 years, we will need four times the amount of all legal immigrants combined. Can you imagine the trouble if our government does not act right, and fast?

Too many millions of immigrants work extended hours, living like prisoners inside this big nation. They live in golden cages without a chance to see their family for 5, 10, 15, or even 20 years. They live in misery for so long, without any hope of legalization. It is about time for recognition. We in America are from too many nations, but we live in one nation, under God.

CHAPTER IV

AMERICA IS IN BIG TROUBLE

An economic catastrophe has not yet been ruled out in America, so you need to be prepared—just in case.

S. G.

If you want the economy to improve you should check these questions out. If your answers are no, we are on the same page.

1. Do you like your wallet to be empty most of the time? . . . . Yes No

2. Do you want to lose some of your public services? . . . . Yes No

3. Do you want to live in poor conditions? . . Yes No

4. Do you want everything to get worse? . . . Yes No

5. Do you like unemployment, trade deficit, high prices, etc.? . . . . Yes No

6. Do you like to buy everything at Goodwill, the Salvation Army, or garage sales? . . . . Yes No

7. Do you want to trade your middle-class status for a poor one? . . . . Yes No

8. Do you like not making your mortgage payments? . . . . Yes No

9. Do you want your house to be taken away by the bank? . . . . Yes No

10. Do you like declaring bankruptcy? . . . . Yes No

11. Do you like to be in economic crisis? . . . Yes No

12. Do you like the collapse of the
    U.S. economy? . . . . Yes No

13. Do you want your salary to
    be reduced? . . . . Yes No

14. Do you want to live permanently
    depressed? . . . . Yes No

15. Do you like American jobs
    disappearing every day? . . . . Yes No

16. Do you like being the next person fired
    in your company? . . . . Yes No

17. Do you like being homeless? . . . . . . Yes No

18. Do you like working doubly hard, and
    being paid half your actual salary? . . . . Yes No

19. Do you like seeing America losing its
    position as the most powerful economic
    country in the world? . . . . Yes No

20. Do you like seeing "Made-in-America"
    products disappear? . . . . Yes No

21. Do you want to have some of
     these problems fixed? . . . . Yes No

If your answer to the last question was yes, keep reading.

Because of the economic situation we are in, I chose not to wait. I took up this challenge to help with my grain of sand, but I am not an economic guru nor do I intend to become one. My contribution is to try to help solve some of today's problems, either in the economy or in immigration. This chapter is just for the economic problems America is facing lately, and I propose a real plan of solutions for the next couple of decades to come.

Reputable economists are predicting the U.S. economy will suffer another recession in the near future. They speculate we "ain't seen nothing yet." They say no more quick fixes; the economic crisis is overwhelming, threatening to put every major city on the brink of bankruptcy. You already know about Detroit.

We know an economic downturn can be catastrophic and crippling to the United States and the world; that an economic collapse can be on the horizon, inevitably to be followed by a depression greater than the last. Some have said that it is not a matter of *if*, but only a matter of *time*. If you are scared about your financial future, you are not alone. We all are, even though the financial markets and unemployment situation are doing a lot better lately. Yet we know Wall Street is very volatile; in 2008, it was only saved by huge infusions of money. The housing market is still weak and unemployment is still high; this alone is bad economic news. Red flags have started to appear on all economic fronts. Our current account deficit is almost $120 billion a year. We are in deeper trouble than the last recession. Government and household debts combined are at trillion-dollar highs. The budget deficit itself can bankrupt our government. The federal debt is more than $8 trillion, which accrues $352 billion in interest.

Nearly two million homeless people currently live on the streets of America, and the numbers are increasing—fast. Manufacturing trade deficit is almost $6 trillion, from 2000 to 2012. We have trade deficits with over 100 nations. The United States has been hemorrhaging millions of jobs in a very short period of time.

We have only just come out of the deepest and hardest recession since World War II, and yet it appears another recession is fast approaching. By giving all the money to the banks, insurance companies, and auto manufacturers to fight the recession, the government took a risk. In the event of another crisis, any available money needs to be spread across all industries in all states. We will be stuck if the banks, insurance companies, and auto manufacturers monopolize the money without giving back to the American people.

Right now it is almost impossible to get a loan for anything because banks are unwilling to risk losing money. To fuel the economy, however, the government needs to make sure affordable loans will be available. The economy is not moving because there is no money for loans, or because the banks want the collateral to be several times the value of the loan. But by denying loans outright, the banks are not making it easy for consumers or manufacturers. They have not yet found the formula to be more efficient and creative, and to find better ways to help all of our industries without neglecting the ordinary citizen.

Our government's economic system is not working and requires great structural change; they need ways to improve the industrial outcome and fix the immigration problem immediately. They can find the solutions, if they try harder to benefit the American people. If our government wants to see some ideas on how to improve the economic input, they can read this book. It is good to daydream, but I am optimistic some of these words will have some traction in industry, in our local and federal governments, and with our legislators.

These ideas are not a one-shot deal; it is help for the efforts we need to make, in full cooperation among government, banks, industry, business, workers, and the general public, in order to improve the economic sector. The federal government needs to flex its muscles in these harsh economic times; and yes, the banks need to change and see how they can be more efficient and fully committed to serving the American people and their business interests. They need to help the working people who are the backbone of any good economic future.

We broke records during the last Great Recession, but not to make us feel proud. We can lay claim to:

1. Record high poverty levels.

2. Record high long-term unemployment.

3. Record high business bankruptcies.

4. Record high individual bankruptcies.

5. Record high foreclosures.

6. Record high welfare benefits.

7. Record high disabled benefits.

8. Record high government spending

9. Record high protesters against inequality in several cities.

10. Record high middle-class families going poor.

11. Record high jobs lost.

12. Record high imported goods made in China.

13. Record high states and cities with shortfall of funds.

14. Record high bankrupted cities.

15. Record high downgrades in credit-worthiness.

These are some of the facts of why the economy has been so bad:

- Too many factories moved overseas.

- Our government spent too much too fast, and not too wisely.

- We buy too many goods and products made outside this country.

- For too long, we bought too many billions of gallons of oil overseas, while knowing we had plenty of oil reserves under our soil and the technology to extract it.

- We spent too many billions of dollars on wars overseas; too many in too short a period with no justification.

- We lost too many jobs at home due to American companies relocating overseas.

- The global competition is normal, but big competition lately has become fierce.

- The construction bubble burst.

- Our trade deficit is too large to sustain.

- The public and private debt is enormous, and it is taking away the lunches of American families.

- There is overly high unemployment due to all of the above.

- There were millions of bankruptcies and foreclosures in the greatest recession in U.S. history.

The economic output is growing too slowly; the new figures are only compared to the recession figures, and these numbers are signals of economic trouble. The double-deep recession will be a reality, if the government does not act. Uncertainty is growing among the American people because of the intransigencies of the government's way of handling our fragile economy.

Take, for example, the deficit of net exports we have with China; it is a huge trade deficit. This is one of the reasons we have major economic problems—China accounts for 70% of the entire trade deficit. This trade deficit has cost us the loss of one million jobs a year—for more than 10 years. We have not paid enough attention because we have been occupied with two unnecessary wars. Now, America owes China more than $1 trillion. So the times have changed: a communist nation is lending money to the number one capitalist nation in the world, and a communist nation is exporting too many goods for not being a capitalist nation. But, we are still at war, and no plans have been made to change or correct the present situation, and we almost got engaged in Syria.

Consider the foreclosure problem. Right now, millions of homes have been foreclosed, with millions more at risk of foreclosure. Foreclosures have quadrupled from 2009 to 2012, and plenty of families had trouble paying the mortgage in 2012. This is not a good trend for homeowners.

This is 2014, and we are hopefully ending the longest recession since 1930. Nevertheless, we are still in a state of turbulence. What we are witnessing now is a grim unemployment picture. America owes China more than $1.5 trillion, and our government has spent hefty amounts of dollars trying to remediate the ailing economy. But, even now, almost every American, with the exception of the wealthy, is reeling under the aftermath of the Great Recession. It has been a constant struggle to pay the bills. The construction industry has become stagnant, working at a very slow pace almost to Great Depression levels. Close to 2.5 million manufacturing jobs have been lost; homeowners cannot make their mortgage payments. More than 10 million Americans are unemployed, and 8.5 million workers are on disability. Disability payments cost the U.S. government $200 billion a year; every person collecting disability is equivalent to 16 employed persons.

Consider the exodus of American companies going overseas. Right now, the American companies are placing their high-tech secrets on silver platters for Chinese factories. We started creating jobs in the first part of 2012, but we do not know if those jobs will last. The middle class has become poorer and increasingly insecure. Some of the stimulus money our government gave to some companies has not turned our economy around. People have begun protesting against financial institutions and demanding better, more equal banking policies, such as offering affordable loans or credit cards with reasonable interest rates. Even after the stimulus money was spent, the poor are still poor, while the rich become the beneficiaries of government protection. More people are choosing to cash their checks at convenience stores because the banks have lost the public's trust.

Consumer confidence is at an all-time low. The experts said the recession ended in 2009; the average consumer, however, knows otherwise

One of the factors that will help the economy grow is cheap gasoline. Yes, gasoline needs to cost from $1.50 to $2.00 per gallon. How can this happen? I will tell you later, but this needs to be in order for the economy to grow fast enough, and for the people to move easily and without a painful feeling when they go to the gas station. This will contribute to their psychological confidence—besides the hard-earned money they save at the pump.

Nearly 50 million Americans are now considered "poor"; all indications show this number to be rising—every day. Forty-five million Americans are on food stamps. American-made products are not lining the shelves of department stores or specialty shops, while more and more second-hand stores crop up.

Right now, small and medium-sized businesses are one of our best shots to create new jobs.

The other day, I saw one of my friends nearly in tears. He told me, "My problem is with my credit card. I spent $12,000 on it to remodel my house. In two years, I paid over $6,000, and I still owe $13,000." I said, "Welcome to the club." Everybody is complaining about the high interest rates of credit cards while the government has been sleeping. People are fed up with high interest rates, hidden charges, fine print, extra charges, and credit card insurance. Banks are not the only culprits: telephone, utility, and cable companies also to milk as much money from the consumer as they can. Calling cards have been ripping off poor people for three decades; yet only recently has the federal government tried to intervene. Debit cards continue to trap consumers: Each time you spend beyond your limit, the bank can charge $25 per purchase, even if the purchase was five dollars. They only pay what you have in your account. That way, you do not overspend yourself; or they let you overspend without charging you too much. Highway tolls also manage to get more money than the toll is worth. Some highways do not have machines that accept money or tool booths, which can result in you receiving a bill for $10. In Texas, if you are late three months in paying your bill, the toll company charges a staggering 1000% interest—even though they call it a "penalty."

While we are witnessing some positive movement in job creation, many of the major triggers that caused the collapse of our economy still abound. Government initiatives, such as incentives for first-time homeowners, cash for junk cars, and programs promoting efficient energy use, have helped us move out of the economic trenches—but only barely. Economic instability and insecurity has become like an epidemic, with only the one-percenters able to afford immunization shots. Meanwhile, the value of the dollar continues to decline as the price of gold skyrockets—now close to $1300 an ounce.

While China piles up gold, American's credit rating sinks. American investments, once good investments to make, are no longer safe.

We need to start again from scratch, and it will take a good 5-10 years in order for us regain our status as a competitor to be reckoned with. We need to start making quality parts, and after that quality motors and quality equipment.

We need to make sure every product coming out of American factories is the best product on the market, and at competitive prices. We do not want to buy a junk car or piece of equipment only because it is made in America; we want our products to be made in America and be the best of their kind.

We need to find ways to lower the cost of gasoline. The Bush Administration enjoyed watching oil prices soar. A new president has, up until recently, done nothing to remedy this situation.

The world is fully reliant on oil right now but the price of oil is too volatile, especially when the supply is disrupted. Iran's plan to close the Strait of Ormus will increase oil prices even further. When a barrel of oil cost $150, gasoline at the pump was $3.75 a gallon. Today, a barrel of oil costs $100—yet a gallon of gas is still $3.75. That does not seem possible, but little effort has been made thus far to explain this discrepancy.

We need to be self-reliant on our own petroleum, even if right now it is an environmentally sensitive issue. Unfortunately, it will remain a sensitive issue until we produce enough electric, solar, or magnetic cars over the next 15 or 20 years. Until we have that capacity, we need to look for alternatives besides electric or hybrid cars.

We need to increase the output of American oil and stop buying oil from the Middle East—especially because that part of the world is very volatile. The slightest provocation in that part of the world causes the price of gas to increase. Has there ever been a time when the Persian Gulf was *not* in conflict?

They have been fighting before Christ, and what is to say they ever plan on stopping?

We can buy a little oil from Canada and Mexico, but that is about it. The banks need to loan enough to make every oil pump available, to put each one to work to maximum capacity. We spend too many billions of dollars by importing oil from overseas when we could be taking advantage of our own oil wells. We have plenty of oil under American soil that we can extract and refine to produce more oil than we need on a daily or even yearly basis.

As long we still rely on gas-powered cars we need to produce what we consume. We could use motorcycles to go to work or we could take more advantage of carpooling; better yet, we could all take public transportation. For most Americans, however, that is not an acceptable option. Yet for every dollar the gas price increases at the pump, it knocks off $100 billion of people's hard-earned money.

We could also ride bicycles to work. One of my friends, a professor at the University of Texas-Austin, rides 12 miles every day: six getting to work and six coming back home. He has been doing this for more than 10 years. Or we could walk two, three, even five miles, but that will send us back 100 years.

We need to stop depending on foreign oil, because the more expensive the gas is at the pump, the more we pay at the pump, and the more we help OPEC countries get richer. Speculators in the New York Mercantile Exchange are also responsible; they like to raise the price of a barrel of oil to the maximum, based on instability in the Middle East. Yet the Middle East is always unstable; minor tension is enough to see the price of oil go up.

But, there are millions and millions of cars and trucks in the United States. There is too much money for speculation itself. We need to increase the output of American oil pump production, one way or another, and send that speculation to a moderate level. Take or reduce any tax out of the gasoline pump, and the government may say, "But, it is only some percentage." Yes, but when the gas price increases 300% that "little" tax becomes too much for the people to swallow.

We risk another recession if:

- The government lets the banking system continue without creating better ways of doing business;

- American companies continue to relocate overseas;

- We continue to buy Asian-made goods;

- Democrats and Republicans do not get on the same page about economic issues;

- We continue to fight unnecessary wars;

- We do not fix the immigration reform as soon as possible;

- The U.S. government continues to give Asian companies billions of dollars in contracts for bridges and other projects;

- The Federal Reserve does not have a backup plan in case of a recession;

- We close schools and lay off teachers;

- Companies let our competitors get away with security secrets;

- The government holds back projects that make up this country's infrastructure, such as highways, bridges, and dams;

- The Federal Reserve prints money nonstop; and

- We go to sleep instead of taking action now.

How much will the government lose in tax revenue in the next 10 years?

How much employment will be lost in the next 10 years?

How much money will be lost to bail out banks in the next 10 years?

How much money will be lost to bail out insurance companies in the next 10 years?

How much money will the government spend on food stamps in the next 10 years?

How much money will be lost in manufacturing taxes in the next 10 years?

How much money will the government lose in the trade deficit in the next 10 years?

How many trillions of dollars were lost in the recession?

How many factories will move overseas if things do not change in the United States, and what will be the cost of those moves to the government?

How much tax revenue will states lose in the next 10 years?

If there is another recession down the road, what will be the new cost?

How much will the government's external debt be in the next 10 years?

TOTAL: Too many tens of trillions of losses to count. It may be the full economic decline of the United States.

Some recommendations for the improvement of the United States economy:

✓ We need to work hard for economic prosperity.

✓ Start financing of "Made-in-the-America" stores and stock them with American-made products.

✓ Speed up the review of building permits.

✓ Build more high schools, colleges, and research centers.

✓ Policymakers in the federal government need to be as sharp as sharpshooters.

✓ Stop policing the rest of the world because we have plenty of problems of our own.

When dealing with economic issues, the decision-makers in Washington need to form a unified front. If there is an economic problem, there needs be only one team—the American Team—not only for this Administration, but for all the Administrations to come. We need to defend the nation, not the political party. It should be the same about going to wars: one front, unified, to make the best decision for our nation. We must not lose sight of one of this country's core principles: "United We Stand."

Government—whether federal, local, or municipal—needs to be well prepared should the red lights of recession begin blinking. Preparations could include having papers ready to approve small loans to homeowners to refinance their mortgage for one year or more, if necessary. We need to be ready to loan large amounts of inventory money to construction companies to create new toll ways, bridges, and highways. We need to stop granting contracts to foreign companies, and start charging tariffs on all foreign-made products. We need American manufacturers produce more goods and to build up their inventories.

In the last U.S. recession 10 million jobs disappeared in just a few years, along with several trillion dollars of wealth. Almost 1.5 million people filed for Chapter 7 bankruptcy in one year alone, and almost three million in two years. Nearly four million homes have been foreclosed on in the last couple of years; more are on the brink of foreclosure. While the United States is creating thousands of new jobs, many people remain unemployed. More than 40 million people now depend on food stamps to subsist each month, with nearly 47 million people—or 15% of this country's population—enrolled in the food stamp program. Some states have unemployment rates well beyond 7.5%, the national unemployment rate. Over the last five years too many people have walked away from trillion-dollar mortgages, credit cards, and personal loans.

During previous recessions in the United States, the recovery came quickly after the government poured money into various industries. Today, our government has poured money into several industries—except they picked the wrong ones, save for the automobile industry. I believe my economic proposal can and will ensure stability, growth, and a boom for America for the next 10 to 20 years, if not longer. To heal this sluggish economy, we need to save Social Security, Medicare, Medicaid, and the deficit. We need to forget about partisan politics and form a unified front to solve this economic emergency and keep it from creating even more catastrophic consequences.

The most important issue in a nation is the economy. Without a strong economy we cannot have a working social security system, a productive government, or available and affordable healthcare. In a bad economy, nearly everyone suffers. Only our government can restore public trust in the nation's financial stability. We have the potential to transform the entire country into a Silicon Valley, where every city thrives on homegrown, high-tech, and high-quality products.

In 1982, I applied for a $10,000 loan and offered an 18-wheeler as collateral. The bank approved my loan. I handed over my papers and left with $10,000 in my pocket, no questions asked. I repaid the loan in a few months and got my papers back, plain and simple. The loan officer knew that with just a few trips of the 18-wheeler, I was easily making more than the loan amount.

These days, thousands of stores willing to loan money if you put up your car title as collateral are flourishing. These stores are essentially loan sharks, and they can get away which charging exorbitant interest rates because most people no longer qualify for bank loans. Consider the consequences. If you have a car valued at $60,000, you can get a loan for $20,000, with an interest rate of $2,000 a month. But in one year alone you will end up paying $24,000 in interest alone. In five years, you pay $120,000 in interest, plus the $20,000 on the original loan. This is unacceptable—yet many accept it because they have no other choice.

As I see it, we have two choices: face austerity for the next six years, or prosperity for the next 20 years. Six years may seem too long, but consider we already have been living in a recession for four years with no signs of improvement.

As of February 2013, the economy has begun to show some signs of life. More jobs are being created; American automakers are showing profits, manufacturing orders are up and the construction industry inches forward; and the stock market is gaining momentum. Gasoline prices, however, are still touching the clouds. We are also experiencing more outside investment: more Latin Americans are investing in the United States; and Europe's economic crisis has compelled its wealthy residents to invest in this country as well. Some economists predict that if we continue the way we are, China will overtake us by the year 2020, then India by 2050. We can prevent this usurpation of our wealth if we act fast, and have a wise and effective plan of action.

We already know what steps need to be taken to reverse the hemorrhaging and revitalize the American economy:

- Stop wars.

- Stop buying "made-in-China" products.

- Stop sending American companies overseas.

- Stop awarding billions of dollars in contracts to Chinese companies.

- Stop borrowing enormous amounts of money from other countries.

- Stop massive money printing.

- Stop government wasteful spending.

- Put an end to partisan politics in economic decision-making.

- Legalize immigrants.

- Improve the school system and the quality of education.

- Invest in this country's infrastructure.

- Spend government money primarily on defense strategies.

- Build public toll ways.

- Re-build old hydroelectric plants using new technology.

- Invest in manufacturing.

- Make loans readily available for those who plan to make or sell American-made goods.

- Ensure our products and services are the best.

- Institute a temporary tax-free designation for American-made goods.

The situation I have presented is dire but we are not doomed. We have it within ourselves to change the direction our country is headed. We have the technology to overcome our economic challenges, and we have great potential. We can revive our economy and restore faith in the American Dream. We can again become proud to stand for the United States.

In the 1990s and early 2000s, I talked to several people in Austin, Texas, and asked where they were working. Proudly, they told me, "At Dell Computer." At that time I thought, oh, what a secure job they had. But, a few years down the road, Dell Computer moved overseas, leaving thousands of people unemployed. The same thing happened with Hewlett Packard, Apple Computer, Intel, and too many other computer and telephone industries. So, in other words, Asia won the first round in manufacturing. But, I bet we can win the fight.

This is just the beginning of the trade fight, and we should not underestimate the willpower of the American people. I know we are down in the first round, but we will stand up, and we will fight back with hard work and dignity. The computers and phones are just small stuff; we can create a lot more than that with innovative and efficient products manufactured on U.S. soil. We have the brainpower. We have thousands of people waiting for real jobs for the next big thing that will happen in America.

It matters that the U.S. government starts with a full swing to help in the beginning of the big task needed to improve the shaky American economy. The banks need to do a lot more to regain the trust of the American consumer. The new strategy needs to be fully improved, so the American bank customer can see a real difference from before. Either the banks do not have enough money to lend, or the people do not have enough money to pay; either way, this is a crisis confronting the working class in America, which bears the brunt of the economic hard times with low wages and lack of permanent job openings.

We are dangerously close to another recession. The shrinkage of manufacturing is a real problem toward regaining economic stability, let alone toward sustained economic growth. The threat of a financial collapse exists. We cannot dismiss the possibility of trouble down the road of our economy, because without manufacturing and the majority of stores selling only products from Asia, the panorama is not too exciting. The federal government is doing something long-term, but there is too little return for the amounts spent; they are being given almost $1 trillion a year in bonds and securities, and not much is happening. They can stop that, and give the poor a real chance.

We are still the rule-makers of the world's economy, but soon, if we do not change direction, we will no longer be able to dominate the world's economy. We have given away, for free, all the new technology to Asian countries to compete against us. Too many new discoveries shipped overseas have led only to job stagnation and decreased income the American working class, adding more fire to the recession.

We need major surgery—an economical type of surgery—that makes sense for manufacturing, energy, and construction industries. Whatever the government is doing is not working; it is not, by any means, solving the economic problem. We still are in economic crisis. Just with the famous banker bonus dividend in loans for factories, the money was good enough to create thousands of new jobs; or, at least to prevent thousands of lost jobs that in the last five years cost almost $500 billion, and counting.

Sometimes in an economic crisis, we cannot grasp the answers to where we are heading; the economic picture is too blurry. Too many economists and economic indicators are pointing to the real possibility of an economic tsunami in the months ahead, or in the next couple of years. American exports are on the decline, and imports are increasing. The new trade gap is wider, more than $42 billion and growing daily. What that means is that the growth is headed in the wrong direction.

Lately, with oil exports, the trade gap is looking better, but oil is too volatile to count on. What we need is strong, sustained economic growth. Without manufacturing, however, it is almost impossible to make any progress. Our govern-ment is in trouble trying to balance the budget; the No. 1 bank is in rough waters; the city of Detroit is in bankruptcy; and the manufacturing of goods is in severe crisis, not to mention unemployment and private debt. Although the lat-est economic news sounds pretty good, no one is safe from future economic crises.

Just in 2013 in Texas, 24 banks were closed. Nearly 6.4 mil-lion homeowners are underwater in their mortgages. The un-employment is 7%, but not enough for the more than $3 tril-lion the federal government spent in buying bonds.

CHAPTER V

THE WORLD FACES A MAJOR CHALLENGE FROM GLOBAL COMPETITION

Everything is global these days; whether we want it or not, the new era of technology is creating a new industrial revolution in all the nations of the world.

S. G.

I LOVE CHINESE FOOD, BUT WE ALSO HAVE TRADE RIVALRY.

China is our primary global competitor, and our rival. In sports, all competing teams are your rivals. It is no different here; only the name of the game is called "trade" and the teams are slightly larger.

China is one of the world's earliest ancient civilizations—and was the world's largest economy for almost two thousand years. China was the first nation to introduce paper money. In addition to inventing paper, the Chinese invented printing, the compass, the needle, toilet paper, early seismological detectors, matches, pound locks, double-action piston pump, blast furnace, cast-iron, the suspension bridge, natural gas as fuel, the mechanical chain drive and belt drive, gunpowder, the propeller, the cannon, the multi-stage rocket, and more.

Ironically, the China of today is not known for its inventiveness but rather its ability to imitate. China has been labeled the number one nation in the world for imitation goods. The Chinese are now the kings of piracy of America's hard-earned technology. They counterfeit anything that gets in their hands; lately, they are not playing by the world's rules of trading, or maybe they never did, and this is hurting the countries that play fair or almost fair trade.

Today, China ranks as the second strongest economic nation in the world after the United States. The success of China's economy is in its population, which outnumbers us by nearly one billion people, and its "command and control" approach. Our economy is politically polarized, going up and down depending on whoever is in power any given year. In contrast, just in the last four years, China's economic growth was equivalent to all the G7 countries' growth combined. Manufacturing is fully supported by the Chinese government; here, not only is our government broke, we owe China almost $1.5 trillion. China has cheap labor and is home to four of the most valuable companies in the world: Nike, Dell, Hewlett-Packard, and Apple. China is the leading investor in renewable energy technologies; and is the second largest trading power with the second largest stock market in the world.

China has the world's largest reserves owning more than 1.6 trillion U.S. securities, and more than 1.1 trillion U.S. Treasury Bonds. China also has the world's most valuable banks, and the world's second highest number of billionaires. China's research and development budget is second only to ours. It ranks in the top 10 countries that have super computers, and it has the largest number of Internet and broadband users. China possesses the world's longest speed-rail network, and boasts of one of the fastest trains on Earth. In 2009, Chinese students achieved the world's best results in mathematics, science, and literacy. Its steel industry is the world's largest.

While the United States lags in college graduation rates, China, along with Korea and India, are quickly catching up. The United States closed some of NASA's programs, while China prepares to go to the moon.

The United States is in fifth place in the world, in terms of GDP purchasing power, and we still produce one-fifth of the world's manufacturing output. We have almost 150 of the world's largest corporations, some shared with Asian countries, primarily China. While we maintain our status as the largest trading nation in the world, we need to put the brakes on the exodus of American companies relocating overseas in the hopes of reaping bigger profits. Chinese consumers do not spend a lot of money on American products, so why do we need to buy so many Chinese-made goods, most of which are cheap and inferior to our own? This compulsion to buy cheap certainly contributes to China's rapidly growing economy and our rapidly growing deficit and rising unemployment rates. Yet by implementing the plan I have presented will stop China from usurping our position as the country with the world's largest economy.

Simply put, we need to stop buying large quantities of Chinese-made products, and stop exporting manufacturers, technology secrets, and jobs overseas. We also need to stop putting American "know-how" on gold platters for the Chinese to copy.

Already the Chinese steal from U.S. research and development, technical materials and trade secrets; sometimes they try to steal military weapons know-how and classified national security information. Some have been caught trying to steal sensitive secret information; others have been caught for the theft of important data and research. Sometimes they steal for the Chinese government, and sometimes for benefit of their own factories. Whomever the Chinese steal for, their attempts are made too often.

Here is what we are up against: Europe has the largest hadron collider. The tallest building in the world was built in Dubai. Chile is building one of the most powerful optical instruments in the world; this telescope will be the size of a football stadium. China is building the biggest dam in the world, the Three Gorges Dam, on the Upper Yangtze River. China already has the longest free-span sea-bridge in the world. India is ready to launch the cheapest homes and cheapest cars. The French are the builders of the largest passenger plane, a 380 Air Bus, which accounts for half of all commercial airline orders. The Chinese and Japanese built the fastest trains on Earth. The Chinese are constructing stadiums for all over the world. Samsung, in South Korea, is building the world's greatest ship; weighing at 52,000 tons, this ship is more than 10 times the original *Titanic*, six times bigger than a U.S. aircraft carrier.

We cannot compete with China on making cheap products—but we can make our products better.

From 1990 to 2010, globalization spread like wildfire and we lost our factories, plus the millions of jobs that came with them. The answer is not to relocate even more manufacturing companies, but to build them on U.S. soil. Foreign governments offer rich incentives for American companies to relocate in their countries; the U.S. government needs to do the same. In the recent past, if the United States invented a new product, Chinese companies bought that product and started trying to make a copy. Products that once could take several years to replicate are now copied what feels like instantaneous—all because we are building too many American companies with full manufacturing processes on Chinese soil. We are making it easy for China to surpass us.

You see Japanese companies in the United States, and our companies in Japan; Korean companies are in the United States, and ours are in Korea. You see American companies in China—but no Chinese companies in America. Competition has become unfair and one-sided; China benefits from our trade secrets but refuses to share theirs. It is like a robber who does not like to be robbed.

We need to stop sending our technology to China before the Chinese government will have the funding necessary to start a similar type of industry that will manufacture products similar to ours—only made more cheaply. Copying American products made with technology invented by Americans is a major loss for our own technological advancement.

Consider this example. If American families spend $1,000, per person per month, at retail stores selling mainly Chinese goods, appliances, toys—basically anything a family might need—they will cause immeasurable jobs in American manufacturing to disappear. The small amounts of dollars you spend can make one million jobs disappear per year. All those billions of dollars making their way to China and other foreign countries is badly hurting the U.S. economy, impacting the unemployment rate, and widening the trade deficit. American manufacturing companies that relocate overseas because the labor is cheap and the profits are higher do not realize that in doing so, they become our competition—and make their "home" country's economy all the more fragile.

We need to find ways to deter our companies from going overseas. A possible deterrence could be to charge these companies a tariff upon returning their manufactured products back to the United States. China may be the low-cost workshop for the world, but with high-quality manufacturing, the United States can be the high-tech nation of the world. Better equipment and skilled labor is the key to ensuring American products are made excellently. Moreover, we need our high-tech companies to stay on U.S. soil to protect their tech secrets and eliminate risk of cyber security breaches. It is like if we allow terrorists to manufacture all our weapons because it is more affordable. Sooner or later, we will be in hot water because they will start using those weapons against us. Even if we make fewer products than our competitors, or if we earn less, we will be worse off if we exchange valuable trade secrets for cheap labor.

China erects trade barriers and manipulates their currency, which subsidizes manufacturing companies. The Chinese are the foremost intellectual property stealers and they monopolize steel and rare earth elements. China copies everything made in the United States, including secret weapons. Chinese manufacturing is expanding, factory activity is increasing, and skyscrapers are booming in more than 30 cities around the country. People have started buying luxury homes, luxury cars, and tons of gold. Businesses are seeing billion-dollar profits, helping the world's fastest-growing economy grow even faster.

World trade is like the Olympics of manufacturing, exception this competition never stops, and first place is not a gold token but real gold. But the competition is the same—fierce—and the same rules apply to all countries. Just like the Olympics, countries with the greatest populations have an advantage; the bigger the nation, the more competitors play the games.

~

I remember in the 1980s when it was mostly toys coming from China. Now it seems as if everything comes from China—but this has led to consequences perhaps unanticipated by the Chinese. Because the demand for Chinese products has skyrocketed, Chinese labor has become too expensive for American companies looking to take advantage of cheap labor, and countries like Indonesia, Singapore, and Vietnam have become the new mecca for American manufacturing. This is certainly an improvement over our primary competitor being home to some of our most valued companies, but it perpetuates the same problem undermining any potential for economic recovery: not enough goods manufactured at home.

If a product in a retail store sells for $1.00, and a similar product in the same store or another retail outlet costs $1.50, which one do you buy? The $1.00 one, of course. There is nothing wrong with buying cheap. If I said that the $1.00 one was made overseas, and the $1.50 item was made in the United States, you might still say, "I'll buy the one that costs less." It is okay. We live in a free country, and nobody will tell you what to buy. You can buy foreign-made products because it is your money.

But, what if I tell you that the more you buy products manufactured outside of this country, the more your job will lose stability? "I have been working at the same company for 10 years. I don't think so!" Well, 10 million Americans who lost their jobs and had those jobs reappear in Asia thought the same thing. Your secure job can be next, if the American people do not reduce their dependence on foreign-made products and start buying as many made-in-America goods as they can.

My biggest concern is not that we lose too many millions of jobs, because we know this can happen. My main worry is that there are almost no American-made products in retail stores, and everyday there are less. Even the U.S. Olympic uniforms for the London Olympics were made in China, one of our toughest Olympic competitors. This is unacceptable. Government agencies should not buy products manufactured overseas because too many billions of dollars go to China and never come back. We do not want economic isolation because we will be buying goods from China—but, of course, less than before. We just need, from now on, to pay more attention to what products we buy and consume.

CHAPTER VI

MADE EXCELLENT IN AMERICA

Yes, we can make excellent products—if we try. There is no shortcut to it; either we produce quality goods, or else sink in the market.

S. G.

It goes without saying we need massive job growth to begin salvaging our economy. We also need to start producing products of the highest quality and at accessible prices. This will ensure our money stays in the United States

By keeping our factories at home we can recoup millions of jobs lost. By requiring government agencies to buy only American-made cars, trucks, machinery, and anything else needed to rebuild our infrastructure, we become our country's biggest and best investors. By consuming only American-made electronic gadgets, clothing, and toys, we ensure our preferred quality of life will be possible for our children and our children's children and for generations to come. We can create a better-skilled labor force and we can return to the time when our grand ideas were implemented for the sole purpose of benefitting this country. The United States was built on the backs of free thinkers and innovators; creative potential runs in our veins.

You, the consumer, have the last word. The choice is yours. If you want to support the American economy, of which you are a part, think twice about what you buy. If the Chinese-made article costs $15, you need to know that only seven dollars stays in the United States, with the rest going to China. If you pay $20 for a similar American-made article that is made better and will last longer, the full or almost all of the $20 will stay here.

When we exported our factories overseas, we stopped producing quality cars, machinery, appliances, tools, and so on. In other words, we lost markets, and that was in our control. Currently, many American-made products are of lesser quality than those made by our main competitors, except for high-tech products. Yet even with technology we cannot stay complacent because our competitors are rapidly catching up—in cars, computers, in heavy equipment, and in all types of machinery. We cannot afford to sit by and watch as other nations progress; we need to do something drastic, and we can start small.

The most important pieces of any machinery (cars, trucks, appliances, computers) are the small parts, made by the small manufacturers. We can start by making better screws, tools, motors, equipment, cars, and appliances.

We have the best war equipment in the world, but only mediocre construction equipment. This is the tragedy of American manufacturers. Those big-box stores so many of us have come to depend on sell mainly goods made in China. There is a simple reason why they do not stock goods made in America: we do not make them. We can reverse this trend. It is never too late to start fresh again—that is the hope offered by the American Dream. We already touched the bottom, so now it is our turn to start using our secret weapons—not war bombs, but our latest technological advances—and convert everything to super-reliable and long-lasting products in order to win back the American and the global consumer trust.

No less than our business owners, our government needs to think twice before awarding billion-dollar construction projects to China, such as California contracting with a Chinese firm to construct a bridge. Bids for major projects should be awarded to American firms only until we have a robust economy again.

Here is an example. If there are a million small manufacturers, and half of these factories need loans, and the banks loan $100,000 to 250,000 small companies and $250,000 to 250,000 other small manufacturers—that should be enough to pump up job creation. Except our banks are in no position whatsoever to finance such loans. What our government has apparently failed to realize is that manufacturing is one of the most critical areas of employment.

We do not want the federal government to loan half-a-billion dollars to the big manufacturing industry; those types of companies should have their own banking finance. We need to help small, legitimate companies prosper into larger ones so they can employ millions of American people in a short period of time.

One important issue that the government and banks need to be aware of is the fraud some companies will try to commit if the company was bought recently. Banks need to look for a proven and consistent track record of manufacturing before loaning money. Better also to loan smaller amounts money to a thousand legitimate companies instead of betting on one company whose only destiny is bankruptcy. We need loans for small factories first so they can make better parts; then larger manufacturers will progressively follow. There needs to be a chain of positive events to be able to put everybody to work again, and this can be achieved. American manufacturers can improve each and every foreign-made product currently lining our shelves. If an appliance manufacturing company sells a refrigerator that uses a quarter of the amount of electricity than that of a regular one, would you buy one? Of course, you would. If an air-conditioner saves you $250 a month on your electric bill, do you buy one of those? Yes, everyone likes to pay less on utilities.

The so-called technical defects in American industry are the faulty components, the parts that are cheap and worthless, and only last a few months instead of years. How can it be that Toyota, Mercedes, and other cars assembled in the United States with Japanese or German parts are very reliable? So, why are American-made cars and trucks not as reliable? This indicates that our cars and trucks can be the best in the world, too, but the parts, especially the small "cheap" and "worthless" ones, need to be better. This can only happen if small manufacturing companies have capital and government support. Better parts may make the final product more expensive, but not as expensive as it would be if it has to be repaired every few months.

Small manufacturing companies should be entitled to receive low-interest loans for "product improvement," regardless if they are paying off old loans. Imagine if almost every product made in the United States—screwdrivers, can openers, etc.—is redesigned to be more functional, thereby improving our exports and our economy for years to come. Economic improvement can also come by way making much-needed repairs to our roads, bridges, and buildings. We can go high-tech on old hydro-electric power plants, fix dangerous intersections and curves, build better dams and bullet trains between big cities, build better seawalls where needed, and so much more.

In order to make economic progress, we need to restart the three most important sectors of a major economic recovery: manufacturing, infrastructure, and construction. We need to at least start with heavy manufacturing of quality products. It is essential to make these factories start working at full capacity, and we have 20 million people ready to help at a moment's notice. With business doing well, the owners and the workers will buy new homes, new cars, and the chain will start moving. Car, construction, and service industries will benefit; insurance companies will benefit, as will every aspect of the economy, like the raw materials business.

The message we have for a manufacturing company is, "You should be entitled to seek a new loan; however large or small will depend on the type of product your factory produces and the number of people the company employs or wants to employ in the near future." All the plans need to be on the table in order to obtain what I call innovative manufacturing loans, or fast loans, for the industry.

We need to win back the American Midas touch. It has been too long since consumers said, "If it is American-made, I will buy it." We will be better if we stay away from products that are environmentally risky and yet still cheap; there are plenty of good products that we can manufacture without causing serious environmental problems. Any product can always be improved, if the factory makes some smart changes to get a better and higher-quality product.

If we rally behind American manufacturers, we will get out of any recession really quickly. If every American bought American-made, better-quality articles, we will soon witness much better economic times. We could start slowly; buy American-made products for one month only. This, by itself, will give us a glimpse of what it will be like when we buy American-made products on a regular basis. I call this the "Buy American Act," and it needs to start now. We can begin with major department and big-box stores, but only with government support.

The government can provide all the ingredients to improve the conditions of the manufacturing industries in a very short period of time. If the industry improves, businesses will follow. The worst of the economic problems will be a thing of the past. The full recovery will be faster. Orders for manufacturers will increase tenfold in every sector of production in factories all around the country, and retail sales will be in full swing. It is just that the people need to have some confidence in the future of the U.S. economy, and to hit the stores and better themselves by buying quality brands made at home.

On "Black Friday" 2012, retail stores saw huge profits. The sad reality, however, was that the majority of goods sold were made outside the United States.

All we need to do to change and improve every product in the market today is test what is available. Every industry needs to check all the existing or dated products—some have been on the market for so long—and see where improvements can be made. Then, we redesign the products to make them better, more efficient, and high-tech, if possible. Yet in order to do this, the government and banks need to put money on the table. Even those who make their money in stocks will become poor if there are no more industries to trade on Wall Street.

Can you envision what several hundred billion dollars can do to this battered economy? It can solve crises of epic proportions, if the money is channeled into the manufacturing industry at the right time. If the banks make 100,000 loans and only 90,000 pay back in full, this will be enough to move the engine of the economic growth. Even if 10% is lost, the government, the banks, the industries, and the people will benefit with the generation of new taxes, interest, thousands of new accounts, and the thousands of new work opportunities that all this will create. This series of government actions will take us out of any recession.

It is easier for manufacturing industries to repay loans if the new products are made better than the old ones. They can employ people like no other sector of the economy. Yet, the government gave money to the banks, car manufacturers, and insurance companies several years ago, and the economy is still sluggish. Not much has happened, so let us give the small manufacturing industry a try.

Do you remember a time when the American people were proud of their "Made in the U.S.A." products? That was a little over 40 years ago. American cars made during the 1920s through the 1960s were the best. In the 20th century, here in America, we were at the center of the Industrial Revolution. We witnessed a mass production of goods; the first car, made by Henry Ford; the first plane flight, made by the Wright Brothers; the first television, and the first computer. We were first to the moon, first in the Olympics, and first in too many sports. We were proud of our high schools and colleges, proud to have a capitalist government, and proud to have the best economy in the world.

America is a nation well prepared for victory. We just need to be the best in everything. Imagine a greenhouse with low-energy consumption that does not need air-conditioning year-round. Do you think it can be sold for the thousands? It can—and we can build it. Our government needs to implement new long-range loan resources for the manufacturing companies in order to improve research and development, to make better-innovation products—along with our commitment to the highest standards of anything made in the United States—and to take advantage of our technology in order to make those products affordable.

In 1980, my older brother started a company with one secretary and one other employee. By 1990, he had grown the company to 5000 workers. After the company started to use computers, the labor force was trimmed to nearly 3000. Now, it is 2013, and still they are doing fine.

We wish a lot of cities in America could be like Santa Clara, California, Silicon Valley—and it can happen. Investing in manufacturing will inevitably be followed by growth in construction, business, travel, tourism, and service sectors. The idling engine of the economic machine will start moving again—this time, in a forward direction.

The government, for emergency purposes, needs to have an employment facility in every mid-size to large city, along with standard unemployment offices that can find employment to any American person seeking a job, instead of only food and shelter for the homeless. The kinds of jobs available in an emergency situations should be something green or solar, and helps repair or replace homes, schools and government buildings—like ultra-light concrete blocks, pavers to adorn the city landscape, or recycling facilities. This is far better than giving food stamps to millions of people who do not have jobs. The United States government should be the last resort for people looking for work.

We have seen mechanical parts that are too old and not very functional. Why not try to improve those with high-tech? Consider a sink. Installing the pipes and other parts are not cheap, nor is a plumber's labor, so what happens later when a small leak opens? If you take a bottle of Coca-Cola and shake it, there is no leak. The bottle by itself only costs a few pennies; our challenge is to make a type of pipe that closes as securely as a Coca-Cola bottle.

Provide a lifetime guarantee on all American-made products, money-back guarantee—redo the instructions of any assembled products as an easy-to-understand possibility. The parts of the product need to be not only the best but the simplest possible (bigger nuts, smaller nuts; bigger screws, smaller screws; easy nut heads to handle strong heads or screws), easy to assemble; less time to assemble, but easy to disassemble, too. If possible, no tools should be used to assemble or disassemble. If an American product cannot withstand the durability of time, at least for several years; or, if it does not work properly or meet the expectations of the customer, change the necessary part to make it a better product. We will not need to sell scrap; there are plenty of cheap and not-so-good products coming from our competitors overseas. We either make excellent products, or else resign to our fate.

Almost everybody can learn skills training. I believe they can learn anything that is required to accomplish a skills training career.

What follows are concrete ways of lowering the unemployment rate and contribute toward a highly skilled and competent work force:

- Offer skills training from high school on;

- Award more college degrees and post-graduate degrees;

- Charge higher taxes to U.S. companies with offshore operations;

- Provide small loans to start-ups, especially those that are high-tech, nano-tech, or green-tech, or use robotics and solar technology;

- Fund research and development of well-known, established, small firms to produce new or innovative products.

- Try to dissuade American companies leaving the United States with higher taxes;

- Rebuild and revitalize American infrastructure.

- Remove or reduce banking and financial services' red tape to enable fast processing of loans;

- Cut unnecessary government spending;

- Charge extra tariffs to foreign-made products coming to America—until the economy stabilizes;

- Speed up approval of construction permits for industries;

- Bring the federal budget down to normal levels;

- Raise the output of industrial production;

- Implement long-term and emergency policies;

- Increase the quality of our products to make them reliable and credible, which is the key to propagating "Made in America" goods;

- Free ourselves of foreign oil dependence, at least until electric and solar cars become more available;

- Lower taxes on American-made products until the economy is back on track;

- Provide governmental aid to increase the productivity and efficiency of manufacturing companies;

- Innovate; and

- Look for the new generation of Henry Ford's, Thomas Edison's, Albert Einstein's, Steve Jobs', Walt Disney's, and Tesla's.

It has been far too long since America was the country with the fewest economic problems in the world.

My ideology is that all the existing components in the manufacturing industry can be innovated by redesign or renovation. I mean, every component in the U.S. market, mainly because there is always room for improvement for every component, tool, machine, car, heavy equipment, and so on. We need full innovation of U.S.-made products to regain respect and trust, to have a competitive edge in global competence, and to develop a reputation for excellent goods made in America. Even though building confidence in American-made products will take several years outside the United States, we can contribute by consuming our own manufactured products. We need to make plenty of high-quality goods, with 100% satisfaction guaranteed for life. The new American products need to last several years, not days or weeks.

For starters, why not name July the month where we only buy American-made products, and see what happens? I always like to buy the best quality product I possibly can, from a screwdriver to a car or truck, and I am happy when the product lasts a good amount of time. But, I am very disappointed when I buy a lemon of a tool or a car. One time, I bought a brand new truck and in less than a week, I found 15 items that were wrong with the truck. Can you imagine what the quality control department of the manufacturing company looked like? My truck looked like it had been built at night and with the lights off—zero quality control. That is one of the key areas of manufacturing besides what type of product is made.

We are in a new technological era, and we need to improve at least everything that has been on the market for some time. There is no excuse for not making our products better than the old ones. Our products need to be useful and reliable, longer lasting, easy to operate and easy to repair—if a part is too complicated to replace, make it better, bigger, smaller, or just plain easy to change. There is room for improvement in every product manufactured in the United States. Everything can be more efficient, beginning with the nuts and bolts. It is about time to remake all the old products that have been on the market for so long without any improvement, and just in time to discover some of the new products that will revolutionize our machinery and equipment, making it so we can build many products from scratch and in a short period of time.

The new trend in American manufacturing needs to be 100% satisfaction guaranteed— for life—or your money back. Manufacturers need to take full responsibility for each and every one of their products. If their product does not last, they redesign it so it will.

It is good for the American consumer to have a reliable product; at the same time, it is good for the manufacturing company to have excellent products to sell. Almost nobody has a problem buying a high-quality product, even if the price is higher than the disposable products coming from Asia. We should be able to do better than those products. One of the secrets of a good product is the parts being used. If the part is good, the product should be good; of course, with good assembly and good quality control, and high-tech included. Cheaply made products have no room for improvement, no matter how good the design or the quality control. The final product will not last, and we do not want to manufacture those types of products here. We need strong, reliable, and excellent motorcars, trucks, machinery, and so on. From now on, American manufacturers must make only excellent products, and consumers must start trusting American-made products, not only because we live in America, but also because the American products will become better as time passes.

Critical components, such as batteries, starters, switches, car window motors, lights, reinforced metal for car accidents, and door openers need to be doubly better. These smaller components are what make a car or truck reliable or unreliable. Some people might say, "Oh, it's the way the car companies make more money, by selling the part several times and charging the customer for replacement." I do not think any car manufacturing company wants that reputation. And besides, nobody wants to be in the middle of the Arizona desert with a car that stopped because it was too hot outside—just because a cheap part was installed in the vehicle. So what if the radio may not sound great, or a seat cover is not the best you can find, or the paint fades too soon? The critical parts, however, need to be 100% reliable, like the key switch that has to start 20,000 times. Reliability starts with the small stuff.

CHAPTER VII

THE UNITED STATES' PRESSING PROBLEMS

Here are the most pressing problems facing the United States faces that we need to address:

1. Fix the economy.

2. Reduce unemployment to almost 0%.

3. Reduce the trade deficit.

4. Boost the Gross Domestic Product (GDP).

5. Reduce Chinese product dependence.

6. Give Social Security financial stability.

7. Reduce the number of American companies that relocate overseas.

8. Increase American-made products.

9. Boost the workforce, creating millions of new jobs.

10. Revamp income tax collection in every State and every city.

11. Minimize dependence on food stamps.

12. Give a chance to every student in the United States to pursue a college or postgraduate degree.

13. Implement a new construction boom.

14. Skyrocket manufacturing activity.

15. Improve every business in America.

16. Create opportunities for selling American-made products.

17. Reduce the homeless population in America.

18. Reduce hunger in the United States.

19. Reduce inequality.

20. Stop Wall Street protestors.

21. Reduce or end foreclosures.

22. Reduce or stop bankruptcies.

23. Start encouraging people to save money.

1. ECONOMY

As we know, our economy was in a volatile state, or recession, from 2008 to 2011. This may be the official story, but we all know by the end of 2012, our "recovery" was weak.

What we do not know is whether the worst is already past us or if we need to put our safety belts on for a bumpy ride ahead. We do not know because a crisis in Europe or some other part of the world could lead to a global economic disaster. We can, however, prevent this from happening by following the suggestions I have outlined in this book.

2. UNEMPLOYMENT

Our government or industry has not yet implemented a concrete plan to employ millions of jobless workers. Many companies have moved overseas; those remaining here cannot afford to hire new employees. For now companies are playing it safe, which is easier than hiring more manpower and building inventory without enough buyers. The financial situation is not easy for factories or construction companies when houses are not selling. We need a supply of fresh money to cover the amount of employment being paid out each week, but no plan is in place to fix the free flow of money. With the economic boom we intend to create for the next 20 years, the government's unemployment worries will soon be a thing of the past.

3. THE TRADE DEFICIT

The trade deficit has been a real problem for the U.S. government, the economy, the banks, the manufacturing companies, and the people in general. For the last few years, the deficit has been increasing to this country's great disadvantage. Hard-earned American dollars are flying overseas because banks are not putting enough money into loans, factories have been fabricating articles of lesser quality than our competitors, and some of the strongest American companies have relocated overseas. This hemorrhaging can be stopped—if the government acts swiftly.

4.   EVEN THE GDP

While our Gross Domestic Product (GDP) is the highest in the world, the gap between our foreign competitors and us shrinks every day. Perhaps one day, the United States will create a robust market for some of those companies to relocate some operations back to the United States, and we will receive them with open arms. We have the potential to triple the GDP in the next few years, which will firmly secure our position as the country with the strongest economy.

5.   REDUCE CHINESE PRODUCT DEPENDENCE

The last generation of American people paid no attention to where their purchases came from; by not realizing their hard-earned money subsidized Chinese manufacturing, they did not see the mass exodus of American companies overseas. It is not too late, however, to cease or significantly reduce buying Chinese and other foreign-made products. As long as new generations of Americans makes excellent products, we will realize we do not need to buy foreign-made goods.

6.   SOCIAL SECURITY

Social Security works best when the economy is robust. Problems build up when we are in recession for several years; too much unemployment means not enough money to fund this vital program. Thus, creating thousands of more jobs will lead to increased revenue, which, in turn, will stabilize Social Security. This will take the worry from senior citizens, who will know that their checks will be delivered on time, and in the full amount.

7. REDUCE THE NUMBER OF AMERICAN COMPANIES GOING OVERSEAS

Once the American people start buying almost all American-made products, American companies will not have to either declare bankruptcy or go overseas. Until now, only these two options were available. A "Stimulus Gift Card," requiring American consumers to buy only American-made products, can amount to trillions of dollars returning to this country's coffers, especially to American manufacturers who will have to meet more and more demand for American products. This alone can give American companies incentive to stay home.

8. PUMP UP AMERICAN-MADE PRODUCTS

In addition to giving cash cards to consumers for purchasing American-made products, we also have to ensure that the product is at least assembled in the United States, if not fully made—from conception to completion—in this country. This will also include Puerto Rico, Alaska, and all American islands.

The more money available for manufacturing, the better the chance companies will have to improve or invent new products. If the economy remains sick, companies will be busy dealing with how to trim personnel, as well as spending and possibly relocating. If their sales do not increase, they will worry about the prospect of going broke. With such problems in sight, it is almost impossible to improve Made-in-America products. A stimulus gift card will eliminate the worries and the problems and give manufacturers, retailers, and consumers the freedom to escape the financial ruts and move forward.

9. BOOST THE WORKFORCE; CREATE MILLIONS OF JOBS

A boom in manufacturing, construction, and service sectors will inevitably lead to thousands of more jobs throughout the country. Imagine nearly 320 million people having the power to buy several trillion dollars of goods per year—this will revitalize our economy like nothing else has. Filling every one of these new jobs could potentially wipe out unemployment.

10. REVAMP INCOME TAX COLLECTION IN EVERY STATE AND EVERY CITY

This is another area that will benefit greatly from the economic boom expected to occur in the next few years. Every tax agency will see the greatest increment of tax collection dollars, starting with the school taxes and continuing all the way to the federal government. Ten states came in short by $50 billion; things could get even worse and spread to more states if the economy does not make a fast recovery. These states need to know help is on the way. Their budget problems will be solved, allowing them to concentrate on rebuilding and improving their infrastructure.

11. MINIMIZE FOOD STAMP DEPENDENCE

Those who receive the stimulus gift card will no longer need to rely on food stamps, which will allow the government to concentrate on those families truly found to be in need. Those who become ineligible for food stamps will have to look for employment—which should not present any difficulty given the anticipated number of job openings.

Today, 44.7 million Americans receive food stamps; in 2008, it was 28.2 million. Most people do not want to live on food stamps forever, and will not need help from the government when the economy improves. Today, one in seven Americans receives food stamps; by distributing them only to households living in poverty, the projected savings to the government is $100 billion.

12. GIVE A CHANCE FOR EVERY STUDENT IN THE UNITED STATES TO PURSUE A COLLEGE OR POSTGRADUATE DEGREE

This will be a golden opportunity for each and every student in America to pursue a college degree, because the tuition will be guaranteed for almost everyone, with a few exceptions. Families with more than four children will need some grants and some loans, but a family with more than four children is uncommon these days. There will be no excuses for students not to finish college. Students can be whatever they aspire to be. Today, thousands of students do not finish college because of financial problems. The children who do not graduate suffer the consequence of lower incomes.

13. IMPLEMENT A NEW CONSTRUCTION BOOM

By making it affordable for millions of Americans to purchase or build new houses—throughout the entire country, the construction and real estate industries will see a tenfold increase in demand for their labor and services.

14. SKYROCKET MANUFACTURING ACTIVITY

With the boost in manufacturing at home, American companies currently overseas will be incentivized to bring back some of its operations to the United States so they, too, can profit from the economic boom. Soon enough, it will be cheaper to manufacture products in the United States, and once these companies see Americans committed to buy only American-made goods, this country will become the "new China," which is just another way of saying we will reclaim our former glory.

15. IMPROVE EVERY BUSINESS IN THE UNITED STATES

With the stimulus gift card, existing businesses will flourish instead of declare bankruptcy, while new businesses will be popping up all around us, like Christmas lights.

Cash registers will ring everywhere. Gains will appear almost instantaneously, for the biggest chain store to the smallest boutique.

16. A CHANCE TO FLOURISH WITH AMERICAN-MADE PRODUCTS IN STORES

It has been a long time since stores in the United States carried only American-made goods, perhaps more than three decades or so. Since that time, we have been losing the trade battle against Asian nations. The major chain superstores have more than 80% Asian-made products on their shelves. Some stores have 90%, or higher. If this trend continues, they will be at 100% in a few years.

Imagine what $12 trillion in 10 years, plus the normal input, will mean to the economy? It will mean more than a $100 trillion in just 10 years. That means stores selling American-made goods will flourish in the next 10 years, with sales guaranteed. The products themselves will be good for the next 20 years, with a minimal failure rate.

So, if you want to take early advantage of this new trend of stores that will sell mostly American-made goods, welcome to the new economic bonanza. The sooner you open the new store, the better the chance banks will be eager to loan money, especially to new enterprises of top quality, American-made products.

17. REDUCE THE HOMELESS POPULATION IN AMERICA

Homelessness has risen steadily over the past 30 or more years, due in large part to the decline in the U.S. economy. The number of homeless people in America has been further aggravated by too many foreclosures. These people and their needs are the last thing our government wants to pay attention to, because it has become such a tremendous crisis.

The homeless, no less than any other person living in the United States will benefit, directly and indirectly, with the implementation of the stimulus gift card. The economy will be so strong that almost everybody will have a spare dollar to give to the homeless. They will have plenty for food, and some additional to solve or greatly reduce this problem.

18. REDUCE HUNGER IN THE UNITED STATES

Some rich people find it unbelievable that, in the United States, many people live in poor conditions, some with barely enough to eat. Families live in precarious conditions, sometimes due to a parent's incapacity or chemical dependency, or because the family's income is not enough to cover every member living under one roof. For these families, food and clothing is always scarce, with no change in sight. Single parents earning minimum wage often times has to work two or three jobs or shifts just to make ends meet. This is not easy to sustain for 20 years, until the kids grow up and can support themselves.

Our population is over 300 million, and almost 50 million are poor. That is shameful for America. Following the plan presented in this book will bring food to the tables of these impoverished families for at least the next 10 years. This is great news for so many hard-working families when sometimes destiny plays hardball with their lives.

19. REDUCE INEQUALITY

America is a capitalist nation, where everybody is supposed to be living a great life, both the middle class and the rich, and with very few poor families. In theory, this sounds good, and is what capitalism is intended to create. This great system was working fine for several decades, until 2000, when everything started to work backwards, and the gap between the rich and the middle class started to widen. The rich became super-rich, and the middle class grew poorer by the year. The poor became really poor, and then stayed poor because of low salaries.

The amount of poverty currently in America is disgraceful for the foremost capitalist nation in the world. Even if the government says economic recovery is progressing slowly, we need an economy 10 times better to give the poor the chance to return to the middle class. It can be done. In order to transform people, we need productive and real assets for this nation, right now. We are struggling in every economic sector, without an easy fix. Inequality will continue if the government does not change its course of action. If the current trend continues, in 30 years, we will have 500 million people in the United States, with 300 million poor, 100 million people in the middle class, and 100 million rich.

20. STOP WALL STREET PROTESTORS

There is an unprecedented situation happening in several American cities. Protests and demonstrations are happening day and night because people have become fed up with the government and the banks. People are protesting against inequality, credit cards with outrageous interest rates, phone bills with hidden costs, cable and Internet services that increase every six months or so. It may be because there is not much work, no opportunities in the trade market, or because of the bank foreclosures of homes.

Most of the time, the government does too little, too late. Now, homeless people are ready to fight silently for their cause; having nothing to lose, they do not care if they go to jail. They protest bank rules and regulations that favor the rich and send the middle class into poverty. These people have already lost their homes. They are peaceful protestors, but they are disturbing the peace in some cities when they protest in restricted spaces. It is not an easy solution for poor people who protest peacefully in a nation that extols freedom of speech but confines it nonetheless

21. GREATLY REDUCE FORECLOSURES

Imagine you have been paying your mortgage for 20 years until the unthinkable happens: you lose your job, and are forced to choose between making your mortgage payment, buying groceries, or paying for children's education. You decide not to pay the mortgage. Letters reminding you of your late payment arrive; as time goes by, the letters become more aggressive. A few more months pass and then the bank send you foreclosure papers. Although you made regular payments for 20 years, and you lost your job because the recession, the bank repossesses your house and puts it up for sale at auction.

Now you and your family are homeless, and you need to rent a house or live with relatives until you can find a new job to take care of your family. You have to start from scratch again, which is very hard for a family who has lost their home to foreclosure. Couples with children are devastated. Families living in this situation are living a nightmare, and it has happened to thousands of American families during the last three or four years. Hard-working Americans are losing the battle against the banks, and with no real government solution in sight, this battle is not yet over.

22. REDUCE OR STOP BANKRUPTCIES

In a single two-period, from 2009-2010, close to three million people declared bankruptcy. Thousands of businesses succumbed to Chapter 7 protection. The cost to the government and taxpayers has been billions of dollars. The folding of companies devastates entire communities; the company owners as well as the employees, many who dedicated years to the company, suffer the consequences of going out of business. The world competition has closed its doors, leaving these workers unprotected—and unemployed. Once we start investing in our own country, our competitors overseas will not impact American factories, and no more workers will suffer shattered dreams.

23. START ENCOURAGING PEOPLE TO SAVE MONEY

It is hard to believe the American people can save money today, mainly because expenses are higher than salaries. After paying off our credit cards, mortgages, and tuition, not much is left to put away. In the last four years, it has been an effort just to survive, let alone thrive.

The shrinking, if not outright disappearing, income takes its toll on everyone. Losing privileges earlier taken for granted hurts in our wallets, stomachs, and brains. Families are struggling to make ends meet; saving is a luxury they can no longer afford. Many do not have the money to send their children to college, and that is very bad for America. Unfortunately, this has become the reality for many families in this country; either they never had savings to begin with or, when they ran into economic trouble, the savings quickly eroded. Either way, there is not enough savings in American families—a trend that needs to be reversed.

If you think I am exaggerating about all the problems the U.S. economy is encountering, think twice, because we were just at risk of another major crisis with the debt ceiling decision made at the last possible minute that resulted in nervous tension for the whole world. When it comes to economic issues, the government needs to form a unified block in order to make those hard decisions that will impact future generations of Americans.

The Bank of America was by far the biggest financial holding institution, and nowadays is a candidate to be dropped from the Dow Jones Industrial Average. If this does not sound an alarm, what else can? The pressing problems grow every year, which only leads to bigger trouble for the already battered U.S. economy. We cannot improve the economy if too many of those problems linger on the horizon. Either our government fixes most of the pressing problems; or, if not, we will not regain control of the economy in order to make it healthy and sustainable.

There is so much to do, and there is no time for political fighting. The government needs to solve the pressing problems head-on. The sooner they put a plan of action on the table, the better for the American people, rich and poor alike. This is just a matter of decision-making, the same as it was for the debt ceiling. This is more important than going to war for the smallest provocation. We cannot afford to wait and see what happens with all these problems—which only worsen as time passes—without a viable solution anytime soon.

CHAPTER VIII

THE PLAN TO FIX OUR NATION'S PROBLEMS

This plan is about plastic and paper to solve many American problems, to make more than 320 million people happy, and to end the economic crisis.

S. G.

The following plan is formulated to boost the economy, and to resolve the problems facing the country and the American people. It is a plan with a sure-shot guarantee of success right after its rollout. Some may say it smacks of socialism, but a socialist plan and an economically strong, capitalist nation are not mutually exclusive. During the Great Depression, the government had to implement a socialist plan to kick-start the ailing economy. Socialist programs exist today to help those in need, such as welfare, farm subsidies, and mandated healthcare.

Before going into the plan, consider these questions:

1. Do you like to see the real end of the U.S. economic crisis? . . . . Yes No

2. Do you want to see more American-made products in large and small retail stores? . . Yes No

3. Do you want to see the unemployment rate close to zero? . . . . Yes No

4. Do you want the trade deficit to be reduced to its lowest level in the last 50 years?. . . . . Yes No

5. Do you think the American people deserve better jobs and salaries? . . . . . Yes No

6. Do you want to see cleaner U.S. cities? . . . Yes No

7. Do you want to see more equality
    in America? . . . . Yes No

8. Do you want the United States to
    continue as the number one economic
    power in the world? . . . . Yes No

9. Are you willing to change your buying
    habits and buy more American-made
    products, if they are available in stores? . . Yes No

10. Do you want a government gift card to
    send your children or grandchildren
    to college?. . . . . Yes No

If you chose "yes," you want a better America, too.

Let me start by describing what this plan will do for all the American people. In a powerful economy like the one I envision, almost every family in the United States will have the opportunity to ensure a college education for their children. The cards will provide work income for every American who wants to work on American soil. A strong economy will help pay for Medicaid and Medicare; it will support the elderly and the disabled as much as it supports the healthy and active. Public and private debt will be paid off, with money still left for saving.

This plan has the potential to start the most successful economic boom in United States history by far; the collection of federal and state taxes will boost manufacturing, finance, retail, agriculture, energy, construction, and service industries—in short, the entire American infrastructure. Small businesses will pop up like magic, and consumers will regain confidence in American-made, excellent products. Banks resume giving loans for everything: car loans, loans for buying homes as well as improving homes, loans to buy land, and loans to help budding entrepreneurs.

It may seem daunting that instead of 20 million people, we will need at least 30 or 50 million workers to surpass our foreign competitors. Although we do not currently have that amount of manpower on hand, we have millions and millions of people who would be happy to work in the United States as guest workers, all the way from Mexico to Brazil, and a lot from all over the world.

This plan I propose is quite different from all that has been done in the past, without any risk whatsoever, well distributed by state, by city, and to the needy people. This money will be spent efficiently in the United States; we will no longer tolerate subsidizing companies who manufacture their products overseas. If the government wants to install solar panels in American homes, the government will buy American-made solar panels.

It may seem like all those trillions of dollars will only add more fire to the deficit problem, but our deficit problems will soon be a thing of the past, as our new tax revenue cascades into massive job opportunities.

Imagine what our economy will look like if the federal government gives each household earning less than $50,000 a year a gift card worth $50,000 for five years, to go toward anything the household wants: to buy a house, car, or some land; to start a business or pay college tuition. Some may try to live on that money for several years, but that amount of money distributed to every household of taxpayers in the United States will still revitalize our economy for the next 10 to 20 years.

These stimulus gift cards will go to those men and women who deserve them: those who have worked for generations, sometimes their whole life, but never had the means and opportunity to buy a house, a new TV, or a computer for their children. Our soldiers, teachers, policemen, firemen, government employees; our all hard-working Americans who work in factories, build highways, or serve people in restaurants: these people are the ones who will receive the benefit of the government. For more than 100 years, our government has been charging tax to every citizen; so now, after all that time, it seems only fair that the government give this stimulus gift card to the people who need it the most—not to the banks or fraudulent companies, just to the people who's sweat and tears have pushed this country's economy to the top.

We need to start big. Limiting the number and cash equivalency of stimulus cards handed out will barely be enough to scratch the surface of this country's most pressing problems. Simply put, the more money spreading throughout the United States, the better chances of fixing a majority of our problems. Conversely, the smaller the amount of money spent on the cards, the decrease of benefits for the people of America and their businesses. Minimal economic recovery will do no good for the country, which leaves us with two options only: prosperity or adversity.

Before distributing stimulus gift cards, state and local governments need to iron out the details, including the number of people eligible for the card, items that can be bought with the card, the number of hours people need to spend on volunteer work; the number of supervisors and managers allocated per city for monitoring the community work, where and when people will assemble to review the process, and so on.

The government will set the percentage above tax that needs to be collected to repay the expenses incurred by creating the stimulus card and disbursing the funds. They will also decide the percentage of the surcharge to be levied on foreign-made goods marketed by American companies. The fine print and other essential materials needed for execution of this plan need to be worked out. Everyone has to participate in this movement, as we would in an emergency. The next five years are the option we have to secure our future.

The best part is that everybody wins, including the government, banks, manufacturing, and other businesses, because, for the first time, money will be distributed to the right people. Every American, without exception, will benefit as a result of the ripple effect of this plan. This plan can save Social Security, reduce dependency on welfare, provide jobs for the unemployed, and improve the economy for the next 10 years, without too much effort by our government. The United States has been helping economically weak nations left and right, pumping in billions and billions of dollars, to eliminate hunger, combat the drug trade, eradicate terrorism, aid in humanitarian efforts, and much more. Now is the time our government helps its own.

This plan will benefit, for example, a fast-food worker who is 20 years of age but never finished high school because he lives with his girlfriend and baby; who, instead of being in school, earns a meager eight dollars an hour, and usually needs to work two jobs to make ends meet. No matter how bright or talented he may be; earning eight dollars an hour working in fast food will make it virtually impossible for him to contemplate the American Dream. He cannot afford to get sick, let alone take a vacation. Things will only get worse when five years later he realizes his family has expanded while his prospects have stagnated. Still, he has no choice but to keep working at a lousy-paying job because he cannot afford to go without a single paycheck.

Many hard-working, struggling Americans deserve to be helped because of the services they provide: veterans, policemen and policewomen, FBI agents, firefighters, and many others who risk their lives for this country. Most of these people earn less than $50,000 a year; factoring in the dangerous risks they take and their increased likelihood of getting killed in the line of duty essentially reduces their income even more. This is reason enough to get compensated by our government.

Teachers may not put their lives at risk the way those working in law enforcement do— but they are no less credit-worthy, and in many schools, teachers and school administrators are, in fact, serving on the front lines. Inner-city schools are notoriously rough, not to mention the onslaught of school shootings happening in some of this country's "safest" neighborhoods. Low salaries for teachers is already ingrained our culture, but that does not excuse the pitiful remuneration they receive. Teachers spend hours trying to educate the so-called "un-teachable" students, the kids with no discipline or self-restraint, the kids that many adults—sometimes their own parents—would rather ignore.

Others who should benefit from a stimulus gift card include the thousands of behind-the-scenes workers who make the government run. They should benefit, precisely because we do not see their work or hear about what they do to maintain the services our government provides for the welfare of the American people. The same holds true for our "blue-collar" workers, those who work in factories and construction, the miners and the window washers, and those who work in food or janitorial services, usually for minimum wage. Often these workers are the third or fourth generation of families who broke their backs doing the same work, all for the benefit of this country. After paying taxes for the past 100 years, it is about time we receive something from our government in return.

Then there are the country doctors, the public interest lawyers, the small business owners, the local politicians—they, too, generally make less than $50,000 a year and thus are also worthy recipients of this gift.

Imagine the joy a small town might experience if 10,000 households received the stimulus card. Now imagine the city of New York, the joy magnified by millions. For the first time in their lives, families will have money left over once the bills are paid. They can purchase a 52" TV to watch the Super Bowl from the comfort of a brand-new sofa, and outside of their home, a brand-new car. Visualize American companies nationwide, preparing en masse for what will be an unprecedented demand of every kind of product this country can make. Manufacturers of clothing, shoes, furniture, appliances, electronics, cars—they will all need to be ready when the American people start storming their stores, their stimulus card in hand. Reservations for airline tickets, hotel rooms, and restaurants will have to be made even further in advance because of the economic boom. No more will cities or states go broke. Every family will have a real opportunity to start their own business, if they wish to, while other families will finally be able to live above the poverty line.

This time of prosperity can happen—if the government wants a booming economy and an end to unemployment; American companies to remain at home; consumer loyalty to American-made goods; increased tax revenue; housing for the homeless; prospects for the poor; money for Social Security; and an end to bankruptcy, foreclosures, and bank bailouts. America's economic crisis can end—if the federal government is willing to invest in its people through financing the stimulus gift card. The government is already spending a fortune trying to revive the economy without any fix in sight; thus it is reasonable to demand our government put its money toward something that will work.

Yet the government will not need to bear the cost alone. Everyone needs to participate—from factories that produce goods to companies that produce products overseas, and companies that do business outside of the United States. Every business will make contributions, whether inside or outside the United States. Charging some percent will pay everybody; it all depends.

For products that come from overseas, an additional tariff will be imposed on top of the existing one. If you want to buy an article made overseas, you will need to pay a certain percentage more, on top of the regular price. If the product is made overseas, the company manufacturing the product will pay a certain percent of the cost of the product, plus an in-store percentage of the cost of the total cost. American companies that do business overseas will pay a percentage of their revenues to a stimulus card fund.

The finished product in retail stores will incur a certain percent of the total cost of each item, and that percentage will go directly to the fund. The same will apply to restaurants, bars, and stores selling luxury cars, trucks, boats, houses, clothes, shoes, and more—a certain percentage will be charged for the fund. Companies exporting goods such as liquor, tobacco, or arms will pay a percentage into the fund. Any monetary transaction of goods through any means, such as credit cards or loans, will incur a surcharge. Bus, train, and airline tickets; sporting events, movies, concerts, and cable TV; phone usage, Internet connectivity—everything will incur a small percentage of additional charge for the fund.

To be sure, this will create inflation. As long as the inflation does not escalate, like oil, we should be okay. The government or watchdog agency will need to look for any company or individual who willfully inflates prices without any reason, like the grocery stores which fix the oil prices super-high without any apparent reason. That is when the federal government needs to intervene. Plus, these kinds of malpractices can be controlled with exorbitant fines slapped on those trying to take advantage of the situation.

We need this plan to go forward, backed by Congress without any obstructionism, as it is for the benefit of the entire nation. Without question, every one of the 310-plus million Americans will have a piece of this pie, the rich and the poor, business sector, manufacturing sector, construction industry, private sector, banks, cities, states, and the federal government itself. Government can work out details such as percentages of tariff charges, restriction amounts, and any change that is more convenient or makes better sense to implement. Major decisions will center around the monthly amount on the card, the number of people who will receive the card, and the number of years the card will be available. A minimum five-year period will ensure tangible results for all the problems. Five years is necessary just to make sure the stimulus card will work well for the economy and the American people.

The greater the amounts of dollars per card, the faster the recovery—and the more effectively our economic problems will be solved. Fewer dollars per card means more time needed to fix these problems. A few may not get fixed at all, if the card does not have enough money.

The stimulus gift card can be used to purchase anything imaginable—as long as it is made in the United States. You can buy new houses, land, furniture, or animals; you can start a new business, pay school tuition, or take a vacation. If a product is made or service is offered outside of the United States, you cannot pay for it with your card. That means no imported clothes or electronics, not even gasoline or food.

If a company in Korea, the Hyundai Corporation, sold nearly $30 billion of its products in 2012, there is no reason why the most powerful nation in the world cannot spend a few trillion dollars to bust the economic woes that have been dragging on for far too long. In a matter of 10 to 20 years, we could have dozens of booming corporations like Hyundai, infusing more than $50 trillion back into our economy through their revenue alone. The federal government just needs to make sure that, after the loan and interest is paid, they stop the tariffs and percentages from all transactions. If the government decides that the card was very good for America, they have the option of renewing it for another five years; that way, they can ensure "Made-in-America" products continue to sell at home and abroad.

We can prepare the labor force by requiring each household that recived the card to work in weekends for a household a total of 50 days a year. We can initiate volunteer projects to make America beautiful, such as cleaning up our streets, parks, highways, and beaches; clearing snow and leaves; helping Habitat for Humanity build new homes; helping communities recover from hurricanes, tornados, or other natural disasters; collecting food, clothing, and toys for those in need; cultivating vegetable gardens and planting new trees—and so much more.

There are many ways to help and do social work in America. People can coach Little League or referee weekend soccer matches. They can volunteer in hospitals, fire stations, and schools. They can finish high school, obtain a college diploma, or get a pilot's license. They can learn CPR or how to learn high tech skills. The possibilities for growth and learning are endless.

Designated managers and supervisors in each city can coordinate this collective effort to better our country and us. This will also count as volunteer work. The size, population, and specific needs of each city will determine how many managers and supervisors will suffice. Ideally, the desire to see our country and its inhabitants prosper and flourish would create enough incentive to meet one's volunteer/training requirements. If that does not work, however, the prospect of losing the stimulus gift card the following year should provide plenty of motivation to get with the program.

Implementing these types of projects will benefit everyone, but they are especially important for those who never had the opportunity to complete—or perhaps even start—their education. These projects will also empower people to find better jobs, and increase their salaries and quality of life. For those who just want to help make America beautiful, their work and efforts will be invaluable.

As part of government-mandated skill building, training, and education, we can also prepare ourselves for national emergencies. We can teach survival skills and conduct mock drills on weekends, so we will know immediately how to respond to hurricanes, blizzards, earthquakes, and fires—even war and terrorist attacks. With a population of more than 300 million people, there will be no shortage of professionals and experts to teach any skill we want to acquire.

The stimulus gift card is a credible plan to lift the economy to high, sustainable levels. It is a solution for a recession, or for a great recession—and it is up to our government to use it. The government must open its eyes and see something needs to be done now to put us back where we want to be: at the top. The government may feel the hurt in the beginning, but if it keeps moving forward, its pain will heal the ills of our economy.

When we start a major building project, we know the probability of accidents exists; some robberies may occur; there may be a possible employee problem or unplanned construction trouble; permits might keep being delayed; a possible shortfall in the estimated cost come up; and other unforeseeable obstacles waiting farther down the road. But, if we are afraid of losses and hurdles, whether trivial or large, we will never start building anything.

Take the Home Depot story, for example. If the owners had worried even 5% about shoplifters or construction delays, they would have never started the building of a construction material conglomerate. They now have stores all the way to Cancun, Mexico, besides the hundreds of stores in America. Wal-Mart has stores all over the world; and if they had been afraid of shoplifters, they might have never started with such a far-reaching plan. It would be like never manufacturing cars for fear they might be stolen.

<u>The Disadvantages of the Card</u>

- People may commit fraud or take advantage of the card; in any enterprise, there is always someone who abuses the system. But the number of those likely to use the card fraudulently is negligible. The government can deter such misuse by imposing stiff penalties for those offenders.

- As long as the government fights inflation like a Super Guard, it will be okay.

- Giving people money for free can have a negative effect on people who subsist on government money only. It is understandable, but those people are abusers.

- People's cards may be stolen from others who did not qualify for the card, but as long as it gets reported in time, there will be no major problem.

Think of these disadvantages this way: just because some policemen in the United States are corrupt, we are not going to eliminate the entire force. There will always be a risk, but this is a calculated risk for the benefit of our entire nation.

The last week of March 2012 hosted the biggest lottery prize in U.S. history: $650 million. With three winning tickets, each prize amounted to almost $216 million, yielding a post-tax lump sum close to $110 million per ticket. Over 100 million people pitched in some bucks, around $10 per person on average; a few even spent thousands, but some only one or two dollars. The lottery organizers said if there had not been a winner, the next prize would be $950 million.

The plan proposed in this book is somewhat similar to the lottery; the primary difference is that for the plan, the Fed will front enough money to give the stimulus cards to nearly 50 million households. Then, nearly 320 million American consumers will pay that back to the government, with interest. Everybody will pay a percentage of everything they buy—this is separate from a tax—until everything is paid in full.

If a family receives the card, based on making $49,000 the last year of taxation, and then, one year later, they make $65,000-$70,000, they will no longer need the aid of the card. If the economy prospers in a short period of time, chances are this family will be making a lot more money than what they made when they started using the card. That will include thousands or millions of households that may need a year or two of help; after that, they will be secure and confident they will no longer need any help from the government.

Earlier I said the government would only need to spend $3 trillion, which may sound implausible, given that 50 million households earning less than $50,000 per household amounts to $6 trillion in five years. But while the government spends $2-3 trillion dollars, they will also collect $2-3 trillion dollars from tariffs, the percentage charge, and the percentage charge on luxury items; plus, there will be millions of people who will no longer need the card in a healthy economy. The government largess will be required just in the beginning; the rest, the economy will take care of by itself. The boom will be so huge the Chinese economy will be puny in comparison; our economy will be greater than China, Japan, Europe, and Russia combined. If the plan is implemented in America, this bonanza for the U.S. economy will be better than if we had found gold on the surface of Earth instead of several feet beneath, even better than if we had found oil under every surface in this country.

One of the most important government responsibilities will be to keep tabs on inflation. This could be done with a special force, a Homeland Security-type of policing. They could monitor the price of products needed first, while giving special attention to and fining any grocery store that tries to manipulate or speculate on any essential food. Additionally, they could impose strict regulations on basic food products—unless there is a climate problem or agricultural disaster, at which time it would be acceptable to charge more for those products affected by that particular problem. Aside from these extreme exceptions, the government should not, under any circumstances, allow speculation or inflation on food prices.

As a matter of fact, all food prices need to stay the same, with the exception of one or two products that might have a transitory high or low value in winter or summer. Most of the essential products, however, should be normally priced, because there will be enough manpower to meet any demand or supply in the agricultural fields or in any processing plant. This will eliminate all excuses for grocery stores arbitrarily to increase prices. The bottom line is, the U.S. government needs to ensure price stability and assume full control of inflation, because, in any vibrant economy, inflation is inevitable.

The following measures must be taken to provide significant revenues that will go toward paying off the government's investment on the stimulus gift cards:

1. Charge a percentage tariff on all products entering the U.S. market from other countries.

2. Place percentage charges on all companies selling goods in the U.S. market.

3. Levy a percentage tariff on products from American companies with operations outside the United States

(except those that produce components instead of finished goods) until Americans make those same parts.

4. Levy percentage charges on American companies doing business outside the United States, even if they do not manufacture products.

5. Charge an extra tariff percentage on luxury items exported to United States.

6. Charge a percentage extra on any sports event held in the United States.

7. Charge a percentage extra on any automobiles made outside the United States that are sold in this country.

8. Eliminate extra charges on food and meals.

9. Charge a percentage tariff for every property purchase exceeding $1 million.

10. Charge a percentage on airline tickets.

The list is far from exclusive; the government could identify other means of collecting revenue.

The following is for the general public, the poor, the rich, soldiers, teachers, economists, police, entrepreneurs, Wall Street traders, firefighters, parents, and more.

1. Do you think $1 trillion a year spread equally over a span of 5-10 years among all U.S. states, cities, and communities will re-energize the economy to become one of the strongest in the world?. . . . .Yes No

2. If recipients of the stimulus gift card spend trillions of dollars buying American-made products, do you think that will boost manufacturing in America? . . . . Yes No

3. Do you think buying only American-made products with the stimulus card will decrease the widening trade deficit?. . . . Yes No

4. If the stimulus cardholders spend trillions of dollars on American-made products, do you think that would prevent American companies moving operations overseas, or bring American companies back to U.S. soil?. . . Yes No

5. Do you think trillions of dollars distributed evenly throughout our economy will cause unemployment rates to decline? . . . . . Yes No

6. Do you think the buying power of cardholders who consume American-made products will reduce dependence on Chinese goods? . . . . Yes No

7. . . . . Yes No

8. Do you think the influx of money
    in the economy will greatly contain
    bankruptcies? . . . . Yes No

9. . . . . Yes No

10. Once the stimulus gift cards start getting
    distributed, do you think large as well
    as small shops will sell more
    American-made products? . . . . Yes No

11. Do you think revitalizing the economy,
    creating more jobs, and improving
    living conditions for the poor will
    reduce the economic divide
    between rich and poor? . . . . Yes No

12. Do you think the stimulus gift card will
    provide a good opportunity to
    address problems faced by
    the poor and the destitute? . . . . Yes No

13. Do you think the jobs created with
    trillions of dollars worth of stimulus
    cards will sustain Social Security for
    generations to come? . . . . Yes No

14. With the economic boom, do
    you think every agency in every state,
    city, and county will benefit from the
    collection of tax revenues? . . . . Yes No

15. Do you think the stimulus gift cards will
    give more children a chance to attend
    college or beyond and acquire
    job-related skills? . . . . Yes No

Now, this questionnaire is for the federal government, the banks, and the President of the United States of America.

1. Would you like to fix more than 20 problems
   affecting millions of
   Americans for years and draining
   this country's treasury? . . . . Yes No

2. Do you believe spending a trillion
   dollars every year buying American-
   made goods will improve theeconomy? . . Yes No

3. Do you think government spending
   on subsidies will reduce if
   unemployment dips to historically
   low levels? . . . . Yes No

4. Do you think the government will save money by not providing food stamps anymore to needy people? . . . . Yes No

5. Do you think the government will be spending far less in bank bailouts and personal foreclosures? . . . . Yes No

6. Do you think banks will benefit from all transactions taking place with stimulus gift cards over the next 10 years? . . . . . Yes No

7. Do you think federal, state, and municipal governments will be in a better position to collect taxes? . . . . . . Yes No

8. Do you think buying power of American- made goods will benefit American businesses?. . . . . Yes No

9. Do you think America is losing ground in the global economy? . . . . Yes No

10. Do you think an era American dominance in industry, trade, and commerce is going to end if we do not change direction? . . . . Yes No

11. If the economy continues to fluctuate, do you think it will affect the Social Security fund in the long run?. . . . . . Yes No

12. Do you think several trillion dollars spent
    in a few years to buy American-made
    products will improve the GDP? . . . . . Yes No

13. Do you think buying only American
    products will enable our workforce
    to perform at peak capacity? . . . . . . Yes No

14. Do you think millions of dollars
    going toward education will increase
    American children's chances to go to
    college and/or become better
    trained to join the workforce? . . . . . . Yes No

15. Do you think we can reduce dependence
    on overseas goods with the stimulus card? . Yes No

16. Do you think trillions of dollars distributed
    evenly throughout all American cities
    will help shrink the inequality between
    poor and rich? . . . . Yes No

17. Do you think the money generated through
    a rise in business due to the stimulus card
    will help American industries rebuild
    this nation's infrastructure? . . . . . . Yes No

18. Do you think our economic boom will
    lure foreign investors into investing in
    the United States? . . . . Yes No

The federal government and banks will fill in the blanks, if they know the figures, because sometimes they do not know the exact amounts. Then, the government will need to analyze the cold numbers resulting from dismissing the stimulus gift card plan:

1. How many trillions of dollars did the economy, federal government, and the American people lose during the last major recession?

2. How much money did the government spend on unemployment over the last 10 years?

3. How much money did the government lose when companies decided to relocate overseas?

4. How much did the United States lose in technological knowledge, trade secrets, and intellectual property when American companies moved overseas?

5. How much has the purchasing of foreign-made goods cost this country during the last 10 years?

6. How much money has the government spent in 10 years sponsoring food stamps?

7. How much money has the government paid during 10 years of bailing out banks?

8.   How much money has the government lost in 10 years of bailing out business bankruptcies?

9.   How much money has the government spent in the last 10 years on foreclosures on loans?

If we do nothing about our economic problems, we can anticipate the following outcomes:

1.   The recurring problem of bank bailouts, companies going bankrupt, and home foreclosures will haunt the American people yet again.

2.   Chances for industrious students to graduate college will recede that will create a void in our future workforce.

3.   Foreign competition will supersede American dominance in the global market.

4.   The dependence on overseas products will only grow at a faster pace every year.

5.   With all the ups-and-downs of the economy, the construction industry will be unstable.

6.   The reduction of federal, state, and city taxes will result in bringing the agencies to the brink of bankruptcy; some cities and states are already bankrupt.

7.   The GDP will be tied to the ups-and-downs of the economy.

These are only a few of the many problems that our federal, state, and local governments are facing, on top of the problems people face in the wake of a recession. Yet by following this sequence of necessary events, we can regain our economic supremacy—at home and abroad:

1.   Congress and the President need to first approve the stimulus gift card plan.

2.   The government needs to deliver the gift cards in a short period of time.

3.   Recipients of the cards must start working on weekends.

4.   The government needs to give temporary work permits to every undocumented worker in the United States.

5.   Banks need to start giving flexi-loans to manufacturers so they can make better products in higher volume.

6.   Federal and state governments must start preparing this nation's infrastructure for unforeseeable emergencies.

7. Banks need to disburse loans to all businesses that manufacture American-made products.

8. Banks need to restart approving loans for real estate development.

Here is what America needs to do to improve the economy by at least tenfold:

1. The approval of this plan by the federal government, followed by the Presidential announcement.

2. Banks start sanctioning massive loans to factories and retail stores.

3. The American people start buying more American-made products.

4. American companies remain on U.S. soil. Those American companies overseas start returning some of their operations to the United States.

5. Plug loopholes in our information security systems to prevent the leakage of technological secrets to our competitors.

6. Stop senseless and prolonged wars.

7. The government must fix the budget, or at least get rid of all waste items on the expense list.

8. Every immigrant living in the United States has a temporary visa and driving license until the immigration reforms are passed.

Collateral benefits of the plan:

1. Students will have greater opportunities to complete their degrees or learn new technical skills.

2. Investor confidence will increase.

3. Consumer confidence will be at the peak of all times.

4. Marriages will rise, which have slackened in the past due to economic uncertainty.

5. There will be fewer divorces, more jobs, better household incomes, and more happiness.

6. More than enough liquid cash will circulate in American markets.

7. If the millions of unemployed people find jobs, they will be physically more active; consequently, healthcare expenses will decline and life expectancy will go up.

As a consequence of this future economic boom, investors from all over the world will want to capitalize on the American boom, resulting in these potential benefits:

1. We can improve our infrastructure and build state-of-the-art scientific research centers.

2. We can retain our lead of the global economy.

3. can rebuild the labor force.

4. We can build better schools and hire better teachers.

5. State and city planning can actually move forward.

All of this can happen—but we need our government's approval of the stimulus gift card plan. If you are out of work, help will be on the way, with plenty of job openings for all. If you are about to get fired due to cost-cutting measures taken by the company, just hang in there, as there will be a lot of new opportunities. If you are skeptical the next economic slump will wipe out your assets, then help is on the way.

Finally, I have two simple ideas for improving American-made goods. If our government wanted to get the economy rolling, they should not tax any product made in the United States, at least until the economy is strong and healthy. It does not matter if the product is a toy or shoes, or even a car or truck—just anything made in America. This will help to increase the number of products made in the United States as well as the stores that sell them and the manufacturers that make them. They will be cheaper for the American people to buy and will decrease the trade deficit. This, by itself, will generate enough sales of Made-in-America products that otherwise would not have any chance to compete with the Asian manufacturers.

The other idea is to reduce annual income tax by 50% for those households that buy only American-made products, regardless of the household's economic status. This would not only increase the manufacturing base; it would also convey to the American people the importance—and benefits—of buying products made at home. In addition, the government could double the tax on all products coming from outside the United States; that way, we will have strong government revenues to help U.S. manufacturing companies in the future.

These ideas may seem controversial, but they are visionary ones, intended to improve the wellbeing of all people in the United States. Yet even if controversial, it should be better than the soup lines of the Depression era, because we know that difficult problems require extreme measures.